BIOMEDICAL FOUNDATIONS OF MUSIC AS THERAPY

Dale B. Taylor, Ph.D., MT-BC

D1360028

MMB MUSIC, INC.

BIOMEDICAL FOUNDATIONS OF MUSIC AS THERAPY
Dale B. Taylor, Ph.D., MT-BC

Cover design: Jill Wade, JW Design
             Images © 1997 PhotoDisc, Inc.
Typography: Gary K. Lee
Printer: United Graphics, Inc., Mattoon, IL
2nd printing: September 1999
Printed in USA
ISBN: 0-918812-94-1

For information and catalogs contact:

MMB Music, Inc.
Contemporary Arts Building
3526 Washington Avenue
Saint Louis, MO 63103-1019

Phone: 314 531-9635, 800 543-3771 (USA/Canada)
Fax: 314 531-8384
E-mail: mmbmusic@mmbmusic.com
Web site: http://www.mmbmusic.com

CONTENTS

ACKNOWLEDGMENTS

Many individuals have contributed in both inspirational and material ways to the successful production of this book. I must initially acknowledge the primary impact of my undergraduate and graduate school professor and mentor, Dr. E. Thayer Gaston, who started me thinking about the importance of biological processes in human musical response. During development of the Biomedical Theory of Music Therapy, Dr. Rosalie Pratt, Frank Wilson, M.D., Richard Lippin, M.D., and Matthew H. M. Lee, M.D., helped provide opportunities for me to test the theory before medical and musical experts in open international forums. Following its first National Association for Music Therapy conference presentation in 1991, it was former NAMT President Carol Bitcon who first suggested that the theory should be put into book form. Prior to commencing the writing process, however, I was further able to test the acceptability of the theory and its components before audiences of music therapists at other national conferences, at regional meetings of the Great Lakes Region of NAMT, and at state meetings such as the Ohio 1992 state conference, and I thank these organizations sincerely.

Special recognition goes to Ms. Sabina Puppo, originally from Argentina, who came to the U.S. to study clinical and research techniques with me, sent vast amounts of new data from various international sources, provided excellent comments and suggestions while serving as a reader-editor for one of the chapters, and has been a constant source of encouragement during the writing process. Also providing substantial amounts of recent data to be used in the book were Dr. Sheila Woodward of the University of Cape Town, South Africa; Ralph Spintge, M.D., cofounder of the International Society for Music in Medicine; Dr. Barbara Miluk-Kolasa, President of the Modern School of Music in New York state; and Dr. Charles Eagle who also provided strong encouragement and inspiration. Others who graciously provided expert preliminary feedback on one or more chapters are Dr. Bonnie McCarty, Prof. Diane Knight, Prof. Lalene Kay, and Mary Rorro, D.O.

I clearly wish to acknowledge all of the investigators, presenters, clinicians, patients and research subjects whose data has contributed to formation of the biomedical foundations for music as therapy. My appreciation goes out also to Norman Goldberg of MMB Music, Inc., who has believed in this project throughout its development, to Ralph Hudson, M.D., who consented to write the Foreword and whose constant encouragement has been a source of energy and inspiration, to Ms. Lee Anna Rasar whose feedback inspired rigor in preparing the contents of the presentation, and to Michelle Adams, my student assistant, whose tireless efficiency helped in the creation of a final draft of the full document.

PREFACE

The biological foundations of musical behavior continue to be explored in attempts to identify common factors in therapeutic, medical, educational, and aesthetic applications. Such explorations are drawing strong and growing interest from scientific, educational, artistic, and medical investigators who are placing increased emphasis on the brain as the most comprehensive area of focus in studies of musical behavior. Even the leading American financial newspaper, the Wall Street Journal, could no longer ignore this trend when, in 1985, it published an article which chronicled investigations of music/brain relationships. The article reported that scientists were saying that, "Music is a window on the brain," meaning that brain functions such as perception, emotions, coordination, and timing can be studied effectively by using music. Since that time, there have been numerous and regular conferences and symposia such as the one held in November of 1992 entitled "Music and the Brain" hosted by the Chicago Art Institute and sponsored by the U.S. National Institute of Mental Health in which researchers exchanged their findings. Although the amount of new research information revealed was not large, much of it would be new to anyone attempting to use music as therapy without having developed an understanding of the brain and its functions.

Perhaps one of the reasons that the biological or biomedical orientation to music therapy has not previously been explored and pursued aggressively by music therapists is that it requires an associated understanding of the anatomy and physiology of the human brain. Most of the research published by music therapists does not reflect participation in, or current knowledge of, investigations in this area, nor do the undergraduate certification requirements indicate that such knowledge is necessary to become eligible to practice as a professional.

Despite the lack of knowledge about brain functioning, medical professionals, music therapy students, patients, and members of referring agencies all have responded with open and immediate approval upon hearing the Biomedical Theory of Music Therapy explained. A notable example occurred following its presentation at the 1992 National Association for Music Therapy[1] conference when a gentleman stepped forward, identified himself as a surgeon in the city of St. Louis, and declared, "This is the way you should go" to get the medical profession to listen and give the needed credibility to music therapy as a profession.

The term "Biomedical Theory of Music Therapy" was first used in 1987 at the NAMT Conference in San Francisco during my own presentation en-

---

[1]As of January 1, 1998, the National Association for Music Therapy (NAMT) and the American Association for Music Therapy (AAMT) unified as the American Music Therapy Association (AMTA).

titled "Therapeutic Musicians or Musical Physicians: The Future is at Stake" in which the need for such a theory was identified. The term also appears in the "Recommendations" section of the written version of that presentation published in Music Therapy Perspectives (Taylor, 1988). Once formulated, the first public presentation of the Biomedical Theory of Music Therapy was made at a Research Seminar held by the Commission on Music in Special Education, Music Therapy, and Music Medicine of the International Society for Music Education. The seminar was held in Tallinn, Estonia in 1990. The theory was first presented in the U.S. at the 1991 NAMT Conference in San Diego.

Presentation of a biomedical orientation to music therapy in this book is not intended to support, replace, or discredit any former theoretical position regarding the therapeutic value of music. It is anticipated that it will provide a common foundation for diverse ideologies, a consistent link between the many disparate and seemingly incompatible theories that attempt to explain the effects of music as therapy.

Prof. Dale B. Taylor, Ph.D., Chair
Department of Allied Health Professions
Director of Music Therapy Studies
The University of Wisconsin – Eau Claire

FOREWORD

In my general surgery career, I have gained these keen perceptions:

1. Good health cannot be defined simply as "freedom from disease."

2. Good health is that state of mind, body, and spirit which allows each person to fulfill his/her optimum potential (happiness?).

3. Healing is an elusive term—impossible to corner, difficult to pin down.

4. If healing truly is not completely understood, all health care participants should have open minds; and

5. When healing occurs and good health is established—it matters not who receives the credit.

The days of solo, go-it-alone medical practice are history—and necessarily so because of the complexity of problems confronting us. Our roles as professionals in health care are seen variably as primary, ancillary, assistive, auxiliary, supportive, whatever. Worth is not to be found in a name. A sense of teamwork has been evolving during the past few decades with the best treatment of our patients accepted as the common goal.

Although not capable of absolute scientific documentation but from personal experience, I attest that surgical patients who are calm and relaxed have better postsurgical outcomes than those who are tense or frightened. Also, from personal observation, from anecdotes shared by others, and just using common sense, music truly is capable of taming that savage beast of anxiety. Dr. Dale Taylor, in Biomedical Foundations of Music as Therapy, has elevated common sense and anecdote to a higher plane of sound scientific explanation. In so doing, he carefully and ably sets forth the unifying theoretical basis for observed clinical effects of music—effects which are predictable and replicable in patients. In so doing, he further advances the professionalism of the music therapist.

Descriptions of neurophysiology and neural pathways, though perhaps technically difficult and tedious for some, are appropriately given to lay the foundation for Dr. Taylor's thesis that the brain is the target organ for sensory input and the mediator of messages which result in physical, emotional, and spiritual well-being.

A personal application: I once had an elderly amputee patient, Ruth, who experienced a massive cerebral hemorrhage. Emerging from what seemed to be certain death, Ruth eventually could perform a few manual tasks, but remained totally aphasic. One day, while playing piano for her in the nursing home ("Battle Hymn of the Republic"), the nurses and I were amazed to hear her singing, "Glory, Glory, Hallelujah"—in tune! I accepted this as a music-mediated miracle with magical and almost spiritual force. Reading Dr. Taylor's exposition allows me to see that what I termed "miracle" was actually "predictable." His thoughts speak volumes about filling vacuums in the world of rehabilitation.

Advances in health care technology are mind-boggling. Who would have dreamed that we could replace worn-out body parts and organs to relieve pain and increase mobility? Increasing technology, by its sophistication, is procedurally oriented. Unfortunately, this orientation, together with the advent of managed-care, has aroused fears of de-emphasis in communication—fears that physical well-being will not be accompanied by emotional and spiritual well-being. Especially now, all health care practitioners should read Dr. Taylor's text, considering music therapy as a planned influence on human brain function, enhancing human capabilities, relieving pain, and subtly developing an essential feeling of control within the patients psyche.

Especially provocative are Dr. Taylor's descriptions of the role of music therapy in pain management and anxiety reduction, critical care and burn units, oncology programs, pediatrics, eating disorders, behavior disorders, and coronary care units.

This text, by its thoroughness and provocative scientific approach, is a valuable addition to our understanding of the beneficial role of music therapy in total patient care.

Ralph F. Hudson, M.D.
Eau Claire, Wisconsin

I

PROLOGUE

PERSPECTIVES ON MUSIC AS THERAPY

S ince the earliest uses of music in society, man has observed that music is more than just a source of auditory enjoyment. The power of music to change moods, refocus attention, elicit emotions, express feelings, and socialize groups and individuals has been appreciated for centuries. The use of these influences in an organized professional discipline to affect therapeutic change is, however, a relatively recent development. A growing body of data is becoming available to help practitioners understand the long evolution of therapeutic applications of music.

HISTORICAL PERSPECTIVES

A substantial amount of historical information has provided the background for development of the biomedical theory. The history of music in medicine has been collected in published accounts and includes clinical, anecdotal, and research findings relating the benefits of music in medical procedures. A comprehensive history written by Boxberger (1962) contains descriptions of the use of music to treat physical diseases beginning as far back as primitive tribal culture and progressing through a number of important philosophical changes up to the beginning of the twentieth century. The long historical partnership between music and medicine from the time of the ancient Greeks right up to the mid-nineteen eighties was reviewed by Pratt and Jones (1985) with skillfully selected highlights focused on specific scholarly authors, research findings, and recent events in the expanding dialogue between music professionals and medical practitioners. Pratt (1989) has also provided a very useful history of music and medicine that focuses in part on specific medical doctors whose names are associated with specific theories, research, and applications of music in medicine, and who have established or presided over worldwide organizations dedicated to investigating the functional and mutually beneficial relationship between music and medicine. In reviewing music and medicine in medieval Islamic and Judaic history, Sekeles (1988) has provided a cross-cultural perspective that also spans the limitations of historical time periods and of controlled empirical research. Also described are belief systems deeply rooted in religious philosophy that affected the medical latitude afforded to doctors.

Nineteenth century musical practices in hospitals in America are reflected in an article by Davis (1987). Selected articles are analyzed that appeared in 19th century medical journals and dissertations between 1804 and 1899 whose primary audience was physicians. An account by Taylor (1981) described musical practices in medicine during the first half of the twentieth century and included experimental research, clinical applications, and college coursework covering music in medical-surgical hospitals and dentistry. Specific applications are described in which music was used as an integral part of treatment procedures in various departments of a general hospital such as pediatrics, surgery, orthopedics, and obstetrics. References to more recent accounts of uses of music in those areas will be discussed in succeeding sections. Familiarity with such accounts should assist in subsequent understanding of the Biomedical Theory of Music Therapy and its integral relationship to applications of music in medical procedures and research.

Standley (1986) analyzed a large number of reports, both published and unpublished, and constructed a profile of the subjects being studied, the types of research design being used, patterns of disseminating the information obtained, applications of music in medical procedures, and results of efforts to use music as therapy in the field of medicine. It was reported that of the 55 dependent variables analyzed in this study, 54 were found to have benefitted more from the music condition than from the nonmusic condition regardless of whether the difference was significant. Such results tend to support the possibility of formulating a consistent and valid theory upon which to base further research as well as for interpreting work already completed.

SEEKING PROFESSIONAL IDENTITY

The National Association for Music Therapy was founded in 1950 and immediately gave form and structure to a widely varied set of endeavors in which music was used to help ill and handicapped people achieve a better life. For many decades, music had been used in various types of hospitals as a form of treatment or to assist in the treatment of persons with physical and mental illnesses or handicaps. Terminology used to designate this activity had been quite diverse and included such terms as "hospital music" and "Musicotherapy," the latter term having been used by Margaret Anderton as a title for a course that she taught at Columbia University in 1919 (Taylor, 1989). With increases in interest, in the number of practitioners, and in awareness among practitioners of each others' existence, a number of meetings were held in which "music therapy" emerged as the term of choice.

With a name and a national association to serve as its "home base," the new profession set out to take its place among other similar professions whose applications were in the medical arena but whose practitioners were not physicians or nurses. Disciplines such as physical therapy and occupational therapy were already firmly established within the medical community and their practitioners were not eager to welcome the newcomer. Although in previous centuries, music and medicine were partners cooperating in the common endeavor of treating patients, modern physicians had largely abandoned music as an integral component of their clinical practice. While some physicians who had elected psychiatry as a career specialty saw a place for music in the therapeutic environment, they considered it to be a recreational diversion or, at best, a way to assist other treatment procedures and perhaps make them more effective or less distasteful for the patient.

FACING THE QUESTION: WHAT IS MUSIC THERAPY?

For those attempting to forge a place of respect and service with compensation through the application of music therapy techniques, a continuing problem has been the name "music therapy" itself. Its unique nature is one in which the profession is designated by its methodology—music—which gives no indication of its goals, procedures, clientele, or focus. Members of referring agencies, potential clients, other professionals, third-party payers, administrators, political leaders, and funding agency officials have tended to respond initially to the term 'music' in the name, and to take less seriously the concept of 'therapy' as it applies to the potential for reversing pathology. Few have been made to realize that the term 'Music' is the adjective in the professional title and 'Therapy' is the noun that defines what actually takes place. When such realization is achieved, it is most often followed by a desire to know exactly how music contributes to the therapeutic gain experienced by the patient. It is at this point that most music therapists have traditionally turned to less than satisfactory explanations in attempts to placate the listener into feeling that his or her curiosity has been fulfilled. Such attempts typically include lists of disability areas with whom music therapists work, examples of successful intervention, descriptions of contents of educational and training programs, and statements calling attention to professional literature.

EXPLAINING MUSIC THERAPY

A major part of the problem of explaining music therapy has been the illusiveness of the term 'music' as a definable entity. It is not a type of phenomenon which can be readily explained in a way that covers the entire range of applications and interpretations reflected in clinical practice. References to music in therapy include uses of terms that attempt to limit the interpretation of its use within specific intervention strategies or to separate it from the broader concept of music as a performance medium and art form. Consequently, it has been classified as belonging to various larger groups of therapeutic endeavor such as 'activity therapy' or "expressive therapy." An example of an individual practitioner who coined a separate term to delimit the interpretation of music is seen in the work of Slabey (1985) who used the term "music involvement" to emphasize the importance of patient music-making in her manual for music therapists. In October of 1993, a conference held in Japan culminated with the adoption of a resolution declaring the existence of a new discipline known as Arts Medicine of which Music Medicine is one component (Taylor, 1993). While each of these designations bears its own descriptive or functional rationale, the proliferation of various explanations of the relationship between music and therapy has not served to clarify the picture. It has rather served to make it even more difficult to describe.

Certainly the need for a comprehensive basis upon which to explain music therapy has been understood by everyone who has ever felt the frustration of attempting to describe music therapy to an inquiring person from outside of the profession by using a good example from a selected population only to have the inquirer ask if those same principles and procedures are used with patients from a distinctly different client group. When it becomes necessary to draw upon a separate set of assumptions and procedures, the confusion on the face of the inquirer becomes painfully evident as she or he searches in vain for a basic premise for music as therapy that would be universally applicable.

THE SEARCH FOR A DEFINITION

In his examination of various music therapy definitions, Bruscia (1989) described very well the problem of creating a definition of music therapy that will be acceptable to music therapists, to other professionals, and to nonprofessionals. Most of the definitions that have been widely used or paraphrased by practitioners have included certain elements that are often heard in explanations of the profession. These explanations include broad generalizations about the goals of music therapy intervention, examples of types of clientele who receive music therapy, assertions relating to the quality of training received by the therapist, and statements generalizing that when music is used in any treatment endeavor, then it is referred to as 'music therapy.' Often included in these explanations are statements focusing on the relationship between patient and therapist, the types of settings in which music therapy is practiced, implications of predetermined effects on specific conditions, and indications of the speaker's particular bias concerning the source of therapeutic influence within the music therapy setting. The latter type of information is revealed by use of such terms as expressive, humanistic, behavioral, or supportive.

What has been lacking is a clear delineation of the therapeutic effects of music itself that would define it as therapy apart from music as entertainment, recreation, or artistic expression. Such a definition must also be sufficiently inclusive to explain the effective application of this one intervention modality to the extremely wide variety of types of disabilities, illnesses, settings, and age groups with whom music therapists work.

ATTRIBUTING MUSICAL INFLUENCES

In a speech to the Opening Session of the 1991 U.S. National Association for Music Therapy, Inc., then President Barbara Crowe stated, "We need to define music therapy." She also asserted that "We need to maintain and celebrate that part of music and what it does for us that cannot be put into words." Although her assumption that human responses to music defy explanation in words seemed a valid and acceptable view for many, this author believes that a way can, and indeed *must* be found to define music therapy in terms that objectively explain a basic domain, a common factor, or a single therapeutic focus that is applicable to *all* areas of music therapy practice.

The belief in the indescribable nature of therapeutic influences of music continues to receive attention not only in oral presentations, but also in the printed media of music therapy professional literature. A noted example is contained in the Foreword to an issue of *Music Therapy* (Marcus, 1994) in which the editor refers to an article contained in that issue describing a young boy's drum beating and his father's refusal to share in that expression. Following an assertion that the feelings of the child are archetypally symbolized in the scene, it is eloquently argued that any attempt to describe in words the feelings and emotions expressed through the drumming is to separate and distort a perfect whole. The editor further argues that the therapy *is* the music, sometimes enhanced by words, which conveys the development of a client's therapy. The implication seems to be that to define music therapy through observable influences of music somehow negates the reality of the already realized experience and changes or demeans a therapeutic experience considered by some to be so personal and incomprehensible that it cannot be apprehended by any empirical methodology or described adequately through verbal discourse.

If the only audience for such explanations was music therapists and other musicians, this may be a viable philosophical basis upon which to proceed. However, music therapists continue to strive to gain clinical equality and move in appreciable numbers into new venues such as the general medical-surgical hospital. They also seek to be compensated as medical professionals in the developing health care arena of the 21st century. For this to occur it will be necessary to delineate a clear and pervasive basis for music as therapy and to articulate it to other medical professionals in language that is technically familiar, medically defensible, and theoretically sound.

The view that the true therapeutic effects of music are so esoteric as to be indefinable has resulted in explanations of music therapy that define this discipline through its alignment with other intervention strategies that were not intended to include music. One result has been the continued inability to develop an epistemology of music therapy that would provide a conceptual framework for the discipline as a whole.

PRIOR THEORETICAL PERSPECTIVES AND BIOMEDICAL THEORY

Numerous theories have been offered in the past for use as bases for therapeutic applications of musical influences on human thought and action. In the absence of sufficient amounts of substantive research describing neurophysiological effects of music, most theorists have relied on using psychological theories to explain music therapy.

BEHAVIORAL

One theory proposed by Madsen et al. (1968) was the behavioral approach to music therapy. This approach suggested that therapists learn to use music as a reinforcer or as an operant to modify behavior by conditioning the client to exhibit the new behavior. This set of techniques continues to be used effectively as an intervention strategy in music therapy practice. It has the added advantage of providing immediate and continuous accountability for the effects of music as the agent in influencing the client's behavior.

While behavior modification has been shown to be very effective in many music therapy applications, it may not offer the most effective modality for treating those disabilities in which the basis of the problem is more pervasive than an overt behavior that can be pinpointed and measured objectively, such as problems that stem from long-standing maladapted emotional development or distortions in cognitive processing. More importantly, it does not provide a basis for explaining the positive effects of other music therapy procedures that do not use reinforcement to strengthen learning of nonmusical behavior patterns. An inherent problem in using behavioral theory as a general basis for explaining the therapeutic effects of music is the fact that the musical stimulus is often applied as a reinforcer *after* the target response has been elicited, making it extremely difficult to show a *direct* relationship between the influence of the music itself and the desired behavior change. However, a clear circumstantial relationship between motivation and awareness of the availability of music can be inferred. The problem could be overcome by measuring, observing and describing the biological changes occurring *during* musical participation.

SOCIOLOGICAL

Another example of a theory of music therapy appearing in music therapy professional literature is Hadsell's (1974) sociological theory and approach to music therapy with adult psychiatric patients. Music is discussed within psychoanalytic, behavioristic, humanistic, and interpersonal treatment ideologies. Attention is given to genetic, psychological, and social theories of the etiology of schizophrenia. In this approach, schizophrenic reactions are seen as resulting from breakdowns in communication with other people and withdrawal into a world of delusions and hallucinations. The procedure has three main goals: reestablishment of contact with reality, opening of lines of communication between the patient and others, and learning adaptive skills in order to achieve normality in a social environment. These goals are reached through four stages of direct patient-therapist contact consisting of assessment and evaluation of the patient's initial status, structuring appropriate programming based on the patient's musical abilities, placement of the patient in a group situation to learn to deal effectively with people other than the therapist, and preparation of the patient with a skill or ability that will allow him or her to be more readily accepted by others in a normal social milieu beyond the therapeutic environment.

Hadsell's theory continues to hold merit as a viable basis for treatment in light of more recent data suggesting a relationship between adult behavior disorders such as Borderline Personality Disorder and social breakdown in the patient's life situation. However, it is limited in its scope of application to only adult psychiatric patients. Subsequent findings and conclusions point to a biological etiology for schizophrenia, thereby indicating the need for reinterpretation of the effects of music within a sociological theory of music therapy. Current literature identifies schizophrenia as "a brain disease, now definitely known to be such. It is a real scientific and biological entity" (Torrey, 1983, p. 2). It exhibits symptoms of a brain disease such as impaired thinking, delusions, hallucinations, emotional changes, and altered behavior. In light of this modern interpretation of the reality of schizophrenia, it is imperative that any procedure or set of procedures that claims to treat this disease effectively must be able to describe its true and lasting effects on brain functioning.

PSYCHOANALYTIC

Extensive analysis of the interpretation of musical behavior within psychoanalytic theory has been provided by Noy (1966, 1967). Wang (1968) examined music as therapy in psychoanalytic theory. Much of the interpretation addressed the role of music in strengthening ego defenses. He also offered psychoanalytic impressions of specific European composers based on their music.

Other work intended for childhood client populations includes that of Hudson (1973) who described the autistic child as not having a developed ego, and the schizophrenic child as having developed a distorted ego. He then characterized rhythm in music as a language having physiological appeal in ego restructuring with autistic and schizophrenic children. Focusing on the ego may provide a structural framework through which to conceptualize autism or schizophrenia in children, although it does not provide a basis for an understanding of the biodynamics of these illnesses.

Our knowledge of autism as a disability has been greatly updated in recent years, due in large measure to the work of researchers such as Martha Denckla (1990). Denckla shook the medical world while presenting at the Biology of Music Making Conference in Denver, Colorado, when she showed MRI pictures of the brains of living autistic children, each and every one of whom exhibited a physically deformed cerebellum, specifically the absence of the cerebellar vermis area. While no causal relationship was attributed, there was a clear implication that further research may identify a link between autistic behavior and cerebellar functioning. Such findings will help to develop an understanding of the biomedical basis for the musical responses observed in autistic children.

COGNITIVE

Bryant (1987) has proposed an approach to music therapy that is rooted in the cognitive theory of Ellis's Rational-Emotive Therapy (RET). It bears a close relationship to a prior theoretical premise offered by Maultsby (1977) who saw music therapy as best applied through a combination of Rational-Emotive Therapy and behaviorism. Within this framework, music functioned as both stimulus and reinforcer for learning new coping strategies by motivating the patient to repeat certain strategies such as rational lyrics to songs. Bryant claimed to have achieved complete integration of music therapy and RET by superimposing the music therapy process onto the cognitive framework of RET. This involved bringing together a client whose emotional disturbance was interpreted as the result of an emotional reaction to irrational thoughts, the music which the client performed and listened to, and the therapist who helps identify irrational beliefs and explore behavioral options. Although the author provided a quote from Ellis (1977) who characterized RET as having a strong biological element to it, he presented his own theory as one that addresses client emotional disturbance as functional and not organic. Certainly the organic components of music therapy processes and their outcomes cannot be overlooked. If music therapy is to become recognized as having a unique domain of treatment, it must be objectively describable, empirically demonstrable, and applicable to the full range of music therapy applications. With cognitively based therapeutic techniques, the organic basis for music therapy is readily evident since the primary organ system for cognitive processing is the brain.

PHENOMENOLOGICAL

Barclay (1987) suggested a theory of music therapy with a phenomenological orientation which adopted a concept of perceptual organization rooted in Gestalt psychology and which viewed the music therapy patient from a psychoanalytic perspective. His work is one example of many attempts to create a credible explanation of music therapy by closely associating it with other more widely recognized theoretical premises, such as was done with cognitive therapy and behaviorism (Bryant, Maultsby, Madsen et al.). The perception of music, herein seen within a Gestalt framework of perceptual organization, results in the formation of melody from separate sounds in succession as well as the combination of other elements into a musical pattern. This musical pattern becomes a transitional object helping to defend against the patient's anxiety. It serves as a metaphor for the feelings and associations that the patient experiences within the therapeutic situation and, as such, can be shared and manipulated within the interaction between therapist and patient. While the conceptual logic of this philosophical approach appears to have merit, its author acknowledges the problem of its abstract nature and its reliance on "invisible and technical" concepts (Barclay, 1987). Although Barclay succeeds in drawing associations between his and other theoretical perspectives, the problem of finding an independent basis upon which to build a concept of music therapy still remains. Such a concept would need to apply to the full range of music therapy treatment and still remain independent of other treatment philosophies. A biomedical conceptualization of music therapy offers that advantage as it is based primarily upon musical influences on brain functioning, a process that is shared by all music therapy applications and intervention strategies.

In stating his theoretical premise, Barclay reveals his bias in favor of tone production as the primary therapeutic agent when using music. The produced tone in "active" music therapy—as opposed to "passive" or "receptive" music therapy in which listening is the main level of patient activity—is portrayed as superior to the heard tone in therapeutic effectiveness. Techniques such as the Orff approach, Alvin's uses of music therapy with autistic children (1991), and Nordoff and Robbins' work are cited as examples of the superiority of patient music-making over music listening in achieving therapeutic gain. What has not been described is the fact that *both* the process of subjectively organizing sound reception into meaningful patterns recognizable as "music" *and* the behavior of actively transforming subjective experience into the objective construct of musical sound expression are operations performed initially by applying the capabilities of one system—the human brain. Therefore, when the therapist is eliciting either kind of behavior from the patient, it is the activity of the *brain*, first and foremost, that is being addressed in order to change the functioning capacity of the patient.

QUANTUM THEORY

Eagle (1985) has developed a Quantum Theory of music and medicine which conceptualizes a mind-body interface between function and form through ultra high-energy frequency control. It postulates an interface of energies between disciplinary sources that takes the patient from the past where he or she has come from, and transforms the whole person while simultaneously projecting the individual into the future as a new entity more in "tune" with the universe. That universe is seen as consisting of rhythms, frequencies, cycles, series, sequences, and similar phenomena that are also present in music. There is an impression that music may be understood as a paradigm for the natural universe as both consist ultimately of vibrations with certain properties. Students of this and related theories believe that properly applied vibrational phenomena may have a direct therapeutic effect on the functions of natural phenomena such as human physiology, and may restore and maintain health in the minds and bodies of individuals with physical and mental handicaps.

The explanation of music therapy based on a quantum physics model offers a new dimension to a very old conceptualization of the therapeutic influence of music. Pratt (1989) reports that since the earliest history, claims have been made that music can heal. While many modern theorists amplify the therapeutic relationship between client and therapists, early thinkers such as Plato and Aristotle believed in the independent power of music to restore "harmony" to the soul and body, and in a close connection between music and bodily health. Modern attempts to use vibrational stimuli to directly affect human well-being have taken the form of such devices as the "music vibration table" or MVT (Chesky, Michel, & Kondraske, 1994); gongs that are said to heal by vibrations symbolizing earth, air, fire and water (Heimrath, 1994); vibro-acoustic therapy or VAT using a chair or bed "filled with loudspeakers" (Skille, 1992); or taped sounds called "music acupuncture" (Hoffman, 1994). While some positive results have been cautiously reported regarding treatment of pain, some stress indicators, and some circulatory parameters, researchers caution practitioners against hastily adopting procedures reflected in these studies. Michel and Chesky (1994) concluded that "in most studies utilizing music vibration [for pain] the results are often erroneous." They called for more careful consideration of variables and more rigor in establishing a scientific rationale for applications of music therapy in pain relief. Vibrational therapy also has not as yet offered a specific and replicable framework for helping victims of abuse, eating disorders, Alzheimer's, or persons with autism or retardation to overcome their problems or learn better ways to cope with the demands of adapting to a complex society. However, improved research procedures in the field of music therapy may contribute to future understanding of human brain functioning. It is believed that music therapy will gain increasing scientific credibility with the brain as its principal domain of study.

GUIDED IMAGERY AND MUSIC

Those music therapists who have chosen to utilize Guided Imagery and Music (GIM) as a technique offer this procedure as a unique method of intervention in the music therapy field. Similar techniques can be found in the work of spiritual healers from the ancient Shaman to modern new-age practitioners. Similarities between Shamanism and modern music therapy practice are proudly proclaimed in music therapy literature (Winn, et al.) and its specific relationship to guided imagery and music has been explored (Kovach, 1985). In this technique, music is used to assist the patient in attaining an altered state of consciousness involving sequential stages in the process. GIM practitioners believe that this technique takes people beyond the boundaries of knowledge of their own inner resources and allows them to tap into and explore a world of "universal" resources represented in myths, archetypes, and mandalas. The mandala is a cryptogram having 13 stages with names such as clear light, the dragon fight, and gates of death. For example, the archetype of the mother may be represented either in its negative aspects by the wicked witch or symbolized in the "positive" qualities of the witch who can guide a person through the "underworld" as well as in the mother who not only fosters growth and fertility but who also presides over the underworld and its inhabitants (Ventre, 1994). In GIM sessions, the guide maintains contact with reality while the client experiences a "trip" into an altered state where that client is ultimately responsible for his or her own healing (Kovach, 1985). Ventre reports that a common sequence of images while experiencing music in an altered state involves encounters with the mother/witch as the client moves toward re-creative images and a state of ecstacy.

While an altered state of consciousness may be quite helpful for some, its attainment through guided imagery with music is unavailable to all but the intellectually highest functioning clients with whom music therapists work. It has not been shown to have superior therapeutic benefit for a wide range of populations such as clients with developmental disabilities who exhibit noticeable mental retardation, children with autism or schizophrenia, clients suffering from Alzheimer's disease or senile dementia, pupils in school who have exceptional education needs, or clients who are physically challenged such as those suffering from closed head injuries, sensory impairments, or speech/language disorders such as aphasia. In the continued absence of direct comparisons through adequate amounts of controlled research, other techniques appear to be much more effective in helping such patients acquire adaptive behaviors, learn activities of daily living, improve cognitive processing efficiency, enhance sensory receptive capacity, and achieve recovery or enrichment of a wide variety of communication skills. Also, the neurophysiological basis of guided imagery needs to be described in sufficiently objective terms to use as a basis for empirical research that would demonstrate its effectiveness in comparison to other music-based techniques in physical medicine applications.

BIOMEDICAL THEORY: AN OVERVIEW

The current theory has grown from a long history of research by investigators concerned with identifying biological components of music therapy. This section contains a review of some of the important work in this area.

PHYSIOLOGICAL PERSPECTIVES

While many of the perspectives cited above do acknowledge the physiological appeal of music, they were designed for use in psychological applications. As a result, the biological foundations of musical behavior have not been fully described and music therapy has come to be known primarily for its applications to the cognitive and emotional problems of its clients. Most practitioners, consumers and professional colleagues in other disciplines seem unaware that a very large portion of the controlled research during the first half of the twentieth century dealt with investigations into the physiological effects of music. These laboratory experiments were done with both animals and humans and they demonstrated music-related changes in cardiac output, respiratory rate and volume, pulse rate, blood pressure, muscle tone, digestion, and body secretions (Taylor, 1981).

When the National Association for Music Therapy was founded in 1950, the original constitution provided for only one standing committee, the Research Committee (Boxberger, 1963). Substantial amounts of research continued during the next decade concerning physiological responses. During that decade and subsequent years, these studies continued to complement the wide range of laboratory and clinical research concerning the effectiveness of music as therapy. The investigations focused on such behaviors as variations in heart rate, muscle potentials, galvanic skin response, pilomotor reflex, pain thresholds, changes in capillaries, postural changes, pupillary reflexes, and gastric motility (Sears & Sears, 1964).

During the nineteen eighties, the fields of music and medicine experienced a re-awakening of their mutual interdependence as each sought to demonstrate and improve its positive effects on human well-being. The resulting dialogue has led to the formation of new alliances, publication of a wide variety of research in which both musical and medical data serve as variables, and creation of advanced coursework and training symposia. At a number of colleges and universities, partnerships have been formed with medical hospitals in order to provide practical training of music therapists in various units such as maternity, obstetrics, oncology, rehabilitation, psychiatry, surgery, pediatrics, intensive care, cardiac care, cardiac rehabilitation and general medical units. Practitioners are being prepared to use music in medical applications as well as to improve their knowledge of the biological and medical implications of music as therapy. To facilitate participation by music therapists in the activity generated by this renewed interest in music by the medical profession, a number of theories, some of which are mentioned above, have been offered as potential explanations for the unique domain of music therapy. While none has been adopted as such, there remains a need for a type of explanation that will make it clear to persons *outside* the field what music therapists offer apart from, and in relationship to, other therapeutic modalities.

Numerous research investigators and authors have contributed to modern understandings of the biological basis for musical behavior and associated influences that music has on human neurophysiological functions. Among these is a treatise by Gaston (1964) describing music as an aesthetic experience capable of enhancing uniquely human capacities and without which no person grows to his or her fullest potential as a human being. Much attention is given to the superior evolutionary development of man's highly complex brain and its hunger for sensory experience in the form of aesthetic stimuli such as music. The author stressed the distinction between man and animal, between intellect and instinct, between the cortical and the endocrine as the principal controlling factor in behavior. The human species is portrayed as being distinguished by a greatly developed cerebrum consisting of billions of neurons, which enable complex speech patterns, abstract thinking, mathematical communication, and substantial amounts of nonverbal communication in various forms including music. The author explains that development of these advanced human behaviors depends upon a process that begins with stimuli that are received by the sense organs, converted into sensation such as sound in the form of music, organized in accordance with the brain's own capacity for processing information, responded to in ways that are rational and individual rather than species-typical, and stored as memories to be recalled in response to future aesthetic stimuli. He asserted that a richer sensory environment leads to greater brain development. The brain with its entire repertoire of coping potential, therefore, depends upon the sense organs for its own development. The implication of his assertions clearly places sensory aesthetics at the forefront as a potential therapeutic modality for achieving enhanced human brain functioning. This is extremely important since all music therapy goal-directed activity is aimed first and foremost at enhancing the functioning capacity of each client's brain.

Gaston reminded his readers that man is a biological unit and must relate to all else in accordance with biological principles. Such principles are reflected in the writings of noted aesthetic researcher Kate Hevner Mueller (1964) who explained pleasurable psychological responses to music in terms of electrochemical activity in the brain which produces emotions as this activity is resolved. Two decades after Gaston assured his readers that the sense organs and the brain deserve our wonder, James (1984) proposed a sensory integration theory as a model for music therapy practice and research. "Sensory integration" refers to the process by which the nervous system receives and organizes tactile, proprioceptive, vestibular, olfactory, gustatory, visual, and auditory sensations. The degree to which individuals interact with their environment both before and after birth, therefore, results from their effectiveness in processing sensory information. Sensory integration theorists believe that a major source of human adaptive capacity and learning is the ability to integrate stimuli from a variety of sensory sources. He asserted that the basic function of the central nervous system is to receive sensory information, screen and integrate meaningful stimuli, and respond motorically based on previous experience. This principle is central to an understanding of the Biomedical Theory of Music Therapy as it is the therapist who elicits behavior by manipulating sensory input in order to control the information that the central nervous system processes in producing a desired response.

Some authors have offered a more holistic view of the functional relationship between music, man, and medicine. Clynes (1985) has described a type of "metamusic" known as sentic cycles as a means of reconciling the assumed barrier between mind and body. The healing value of music is portrayed in its ability to provide a means for expression of essentic form, which is defined as a biologically given form of expression for a specific emotion. Because emotional awareness is afforded by release of neurochemical substances in the brain, it is possible to use music to stimulate biochemical changes within the human brain according to this theory. Another example of an extensive review of the relationship between music and the human body was presented by Verdeau-Pailles (1985). Her work offers explanations for relationships between musical elements such as melody, rhythm and dynamics and normal biological processes within the human organism. Other factors found in music such as tension, relaxation, silence, improvisation and creativity are also described as having parallels in the dynamics of basic human biological functioning. An understanding of biomedical theory would be enhanced by some familiarity with these parallels.

Students of psychomusicology have begun to seek answers to questions about control of the human neuromuscular system during musical performance, and about the relationship between brain activity, music cognition, and their medical implications. Both Wilson (1988) and Manchester (1988) have described the current picture concerning the implications of the biological processes involved in music making for medical applications in treating persons with disorders involving those same processes. Included are medical problems arising from music making as well as the use of music to treat other physical problems that share biological functions with musical behaviors. Wilson (1985) suggested that music and medicine "are close to a rediscovery of their traditional bonds." The biomedical theory is intended to provide a practical foundation for professionals in both music and in medicine to proceed with research and clinical applications of music in medical procedures. Upon hearing the biomedical theory presented, physicians have repeatedly asserted that knowledge of this theory would prompt the medical profession to listen and give the needed credibility to music therapy as a professional discipline.

THE BIOMEDICAL PERSPECTIVE

The purpose of the present work is to describe a theory of music therapy that will provide a practical and useful foundation for research and applications of music in medicine. When properly applied, it provides a strong basis for clinical practice, and may also generate the type of data needed by third party payers to fund music therapy intervention both within medical and more traditional clinical and educational settings. This approach is unlike other theories which have been proposed in the past primarily for use with psychiatric and developmentally disabled clients. It is called the Biomedical Theory of Music Therapy, a term first used in 1987 at the NAMT Conference in San Francisco during a presentation entitled "Therapeutic Musicians or Musical Physicians: The Future is at Stake" in which the need for such a framework was identified.

In the present work, the Biomedical Theory of Music Therapy with its four subtheories is offered as an independent basis for music therapy practice, research and definition. This theory systematically and objectively defines music therapy interventions in terms that are applicable to the full range of client populations served. It establishes the human brain as the basic domain of treatment and the primary focus for change in all music therapy applications. The basic theory holds that because music has observable effects on human brain functioning, its effects can be used therapeutically. The four hypotheses deal with the neurological pathways for the effect of music on pain, neural processing of musical stimuli in cranial centers for emotion, physiological responses to music associated with communication and movement, and musical influences on anxiety and stress physiology.

Each of the four hypotheses is examined in a separate chapter. A thorough examination of the central place of the brain in music therapy is included in the following chapter.

II

THE HUMAN BRAIN

THE TRUE DOMAIN
OF MUSIC THERAPY

S cholars in the neurosciences have reported that "all human behavior is generated by the brain" (Hodges, 1980b). This statement indicates that there is an almost incomprehensible number of behavioral capabilities that could be produced from at least 10 trillion known connections between neurons in the human brain. It also makes it incumbent upon students of any type of human behavior to study and become thoroughly familiar with the brain as it affects their domain. This injunction certainly would apply to anyone who studies music as therapy in medical and medically related procedures.

BRAIN FUNCTIONING:
THE KEY TO UNDERSTANDING MUSIC THERAPY

Investigations of music/brain relationships provide the means for describing therapeutic influences of music in terms that explain objectively a basic domain, a single theoretical framework, that applies to *all* music therapy applications. Many supporters and practitioners of music therapy are developing an intimate level of knowledge with the information being exchanged. In a speech to an audience of music therapists, Mathew Lee, M.D., head of the Rusk Institute of Rehabilitation Medicine in New York City, advised his listeners to "Forget all this psychology stuff and get on with music as medicine." This is interpreted to mean that music therapists should find a medical basis for musical interventions that is independent of other psychological intervention strategies. Such a foundation must be applicable to all music therapy practices and will gain its credibility by demonstrating its ability to be observed empirically.

It is now quite evident that the point of primary interest in the search for a universal domain of music therapy should be the brain. This clear conclusion is based on the inescapable fact that literally all of the work that music therapists do is primarily and ultimately aimed at changing the functions of specific biological structures of the human body. Such change *begins* with the brain which must interpret any sound as "music" before that sound can exert a "musical" influence. For example, when treating psychiatric disorders whether schizophrenic, borderline, bipolar, or any one of numerous other behavior disorders, the principal locus of the problem is in the client's *brain*. Also, with cognitive impairments in psychiatric or developmental disorders, it is the ability of the brain to process information and direct appropriate coping responses that determines the goals of the music therapist. In general hospital applications one of the most widespread uses of music is to decrease pain perception by raising the threshold of pain stimuli reaching somatosensory portions of the patient's brain.

The growing number of music therapists whose positions are in the nursing home/extended care industry are working daily to combat the effects of Alzheimer's disease, arteriosclerosis, and cardiovascular diseases such as strokes which have a profound effect on the patient's brain. These brain diseases also have corresponding effects on other biological systems such as the circulatory and muscle systems. Clients whose handicaps are physical in nature receive music therapy intervention designed to improve physical functioning, a class of behavior which itself is totally dependent upon motivation and neurological control originating in the brain. One of the more frequently seen physical handicaps, cerebral palsy, receives its *name* from its source, the brain. Intervention with clients having sensory disorders centers around helping find ways to maximize the availability of environmental information accessible to the brain. Those exhibiting communication disorders such as aphasia receive music therapy treatment designed to utilize the functional plasticity of the human brain as it compensates for processing and muscular innervation capabilities lost due to lesions or other brain damage. Closer examination of musical influences on brain processing in clients having these and related disorders is contained in subsequent chapters.

UNDERSTANDING THERAPEUTIC EFFECTS OF MUSIC ON THE BRAIN

In order to understand and utilize biomedical theory in music therapy, it is necessary that the practitioner have some familiarity with basic neurophysiology, brain pathology, and perhaps neuromusicology, psychomusicology, neuroimmunology, neurochemistry, and physiological psychology. Use of a biologically based theory of music therapy and the emerging body of literature describing human brain function requires increased understanding of the brain. For example, responses to music that were formerly assumed to be beyond verbal description are being placed into a workable framework as theorists become familiar with basic conceptualizations of human brain functioning.

Harvey (1987) reviewed a large amount of activity in the fields of music and medicine that tends to point toward much greater convergence of the two fields. He cited numerous clinical research studies indicating that music does have a predictable effect on human behavior during medical procedures. An institute for further study of the music-mind-medicine relationship was proposed, based in part on the following three assumptions which parallel basic tenets of the Biomedical Theory of Music Therapy.

a. The center of control for the human organism is the brain.

b. Music is processed by the brain and through the brain, after which it can then affect us in many ways.

c. Music can have a positive effect upon both neural functions and hormonal activity and, as such, can facilitate the healthy functioning of the body's own immune and regenerative processes (Harvey, 1987, p. 73–74).

By viewing music therapy from the perspective of biological functioning, it should no longer be necessary to refer to the therapeutic influences of music as magical, mystical, or unexplainable. For example, Chapter 7 contains a thorough neurophysiological explanation of the immune system's response to music. In order to fully comprehend the nature and structure of biomedical theory, it is necessary to begin with an understanding of the auditory sensory/

perceptual system including its importance to human brain functioning and its ability to interface with those systems that govern other domains of human behavior. The next section will explore these three prerequisite areas.

DEVELOPMENTAL AUDIATION AND MUSIC

PRENATAL AUDITORY DEVELOPMENT AND MUSIC

Gaston (1968) contended that the senses provide humans with the basic material that is needed to create intelligence. Because humans lack any appreciable opportunity to rely on instinct for survival, the human brain must constantly generate rationally determined decisions in order to cope with the environment outside of the body. Development of this ability is constantly and totally dependent upon the senses for information to be processed. In fact, the brain does not react favorably to any lapse in the flow of sensory input, which partially explains man's motivation to produce stimuli in the form of aesthetic expression for the pure pleasure of sensory enjoyment. It is this innate hunger in every patient's brain for aesthetic stimulation that is a major factor in explaining why music, as an aesthetic experience, is so universally applicable to the treatment of such a wide variety of human conditions.

The ears, eyes, skin receptors, tongue, and nose are the end organs of human senses. They send the information that they receive to only one place, the brain. The brain, in turn, is totally dependent upon the senses for information about the surrounding environment. It must, therefore, depend upon the senses for stimuli that it will process to both determine immediate responses and develop overall intelligence. Because the newborn baby arrives already able to exhibit some sensory response capabilities that require substantial brain development, the inevitable question arises: How and when did the brain begin to develop those abilities?

The answer to the 'when' portion of the above question can be determined only by examining fetal perceptual development. There is no evidence that the visual, tactual, olfactory, gustatory, or kinesthetic fields of intrauterine stimuli are sufficiently rich to account for development of the kinds of responsive abilities evident in the neonate at birth. Intrauterine experiences in those sensory pathways also have not been shown to be sufficient to support an assumption that they helped provide a foundation for rapid acceleration in the learning curve observable in infant behavior. By contrast, the early appearance of auditory receptors, responses of the fetus to auditory and vibroacoustic stimuli, and the substantial amount and variety of information in the intrauterine acoustic environment indicate that the auditory tract may well be the fetal brain's primary source of stimulation for formation of the cognitive structures to be used initially for postnatal intellectual development. How the brain developed its capacities will become evident by determining when and to what extent acquisition of various sensory responses occurred.

The evidence shows that the ear first appears 22 days into gestation. According to Panthuraamphorn (1993), "many studies demonstrate that the fetus can perceive auditory stimulation even in the first trimester of pregnancy" (p. 192). However, structural maturation of the most intricate aspects of the human hearing mechanism indicate actual hearing functions appear at about 25 weeks (nearly six months) of gestation (Woodward et al., 1992). Cochlear function, basilar membrane response, and development of both inner and outer rows of hair cells all appear by the fifth to the seventh month permitting transmission of encoded acoustic information to the eighth cranial nerve, which is the first of the cranial nerves to develop in the fetal brain. Research showing auditory evoked response in the fetal brain shows that the stimulus is transmitted to the brain where it can be perceived and stored in memory (Shetler, 1990).

It is important to differentiate here between the three principle types of stimulation used to test fetal responses. Vibroacoustic stimuli (VS) consist of periodic pure or complex single tones of a given frequency presented for two or more seconds at various intensity levels. Tones are generated using a battery-powered artificial larynx designed to minimize the effects of impedance as vibrations pass through tissue and fluid. Studies showing no response in anencephalic fetuses support the interpretation of a cochlear rather than a cutaneous response to VS (Woodward, 1992).

Another form of stimulation, acoustic stimuli (AS), utilizes single pure tones above 800 Hz in order to exclude tangible vibration. Reactions of the fetus to external sensory stimuli can be measured using heart rate variations, changes in electromagnetic brain activity, or bodily movement patterns (Panthuraamphorn, 1993). The behavioral parameter of choice in studies of responses to AS is fetal heart rate (FHR) which has been shown to be immediately responsive in a vast majority of fetuses studied. The Auditory Stimulation Test (AST) has been shown to be even more sensitive for apprehension of fetal compromise than the more traditionally used nonstress test (NST). The AST takes much less time to administer than the NST and it has decreased by nearly 50% the number of nonreactive tests. Studies have shown that normal third trimester fetal response to VS and AS is so consistent that the AST is now used commonly in measuring fetal well-being (Woodward, 1992).

The third type of stimulation used to test fetal responses is music. When music is played to the mother via headphones, no response is detected in the fetus. However, when headphones are placed on the mother's abdomen allowing the music to go directly to the fetus, FHR changes are observed consistently. FHR accelerations and limb movements in response to piano and choral music are reliably observed at 38 weeks. Research in this area indicates that music not only penetrates the uterus, but that "the normal third-trimester fetus perceives and responds to external music stimuli" (Woodward et al., 1992, p. 62). It was also concluded that music presented repeatedly during the intrauterine stage is more reinforcing for the postnatal behavior of the neonate than music that has not been previously presented. This finding was supported by Panthuraamphorn (1993) who reported that newborns who have been sung to prenatally appear calm, attentive and highly alert to their new environment in the immediate postnatal period. Melodic voices and classical music were recommended as adequate auditory stimuli, whereas unharmonic and loud sounds were identified as stimuli to be avoided.

MUSIC

Before progressing further into prenatal-postnatal processing of music and effects of music on the brain, it is important to clarify what type of auditory stimuli are referred to as "music" by this author. Herein, music should be understood to mean a series of sounds that are created with the intent of aesthetic expression and are accepted as representative of the concept of music within the cultural context. This conceptualization of music is intended to clarify its meaning as an expressive and perceptual modality when used in the term "Music Therapy" in this book. In some instances however, data on the effects of other types of sound organization (e.g., a single steady frequency) has been included and the alternative types of extramusical stimuli have been specified. It should be clear to the reader that this author believes that references to such uses of sound stimulation must not be confused with legitimate applications of music as therapy.

DEVELOPMENTAL FUNCTIONS OF PRENATAL MUSIC AUDIATION

When music or other auditory stimuli reach the fetal brain, they are received as sensations rather than simply as patterns of nerve impulses. Sensation is a prerequisite to perception and makes information available from the external environment. This information is then processed in the full operation known as perception, which includes identification and labeling, comparison to previously received sensations, contextual identification, and memory storage for subsequent recall. Through perception, the brain seeks similarity, context, forms and patterns from sensory data. The effect of such fetal brain activity is that the development of uniquely human brain capacity begins long before the child is born. The amazingly rapid mental progress in human babies can therefore be accounted for by the prenatal sensory experiences that build and install in the brain certain cognitive structures which are ready at birth to receive and perceive sensory data, process perception, and shape experience (Ward, 1993). It is this need and ability of the patient's brain to apply cognition to perception that the music therapist seeks to utilize when eliciting musically structured responses during therapy. Through musical procedures designed to help the patient develop or redevelop such ability, the therapy progresses toward improved performance in the *brain*, which makes the brain the true domain of the music therapist.

Theorists have noted the salient feature that distinguishes man is the comparative complexity and elaboration of the human brain and the tremendous variety of responses of which it is capable. Becoming human means, for example, acquisition of articulate speech, abstract thinking, and mathematical computation. Brain development, however, is dependent upon sensory stimulation and the greater the sensory environment, the greater the brain development (Gaston, 1964). To some prominent theorists, the single most distinguishing human capability is speech communication which involves auditory sensation and related systems (Roederer, 1985). There is no equivalent expressive mode corresponding to any of the other senses. Many consider verbal communication to be more important than vision, e.g., without special training a blind person can converse with greater ease than a deaf person can; acoustic stimuli also inform about phenomena that are hidden from view by obstructions or by darkness (Carlson, 1992).

A substantial amount of speculation has been devoted to determining the function of musical behavior in humans, especially as compared to the absence of purely aesthetic expression in other animal species. Dr. Norman Weinberger (1993), Scientific Director of the Music Brain Information Center at the University of California, Irvine, has concluded that findings from studies of the evoked magnetic responses of cells in the auditory cortex reveal that a basic capacity for auditory perception was established in evolution to process those aspects of sound that are basically musical in nature, and that this supports the idea that music is far more than a social diversion—it may be a biological imperative. It is now widely agreed that musical stimulation via both instrumental and vocal music positively influences the brain both prenatally and postnatally (Babic, 1993).

Much of the attention concerning the innate function of music has focused on the latest research in language acquisition. This research indicates that the ability for meaningful processing of acoustical nuances is generated in the human brain during embryonic development (Ostwald, 1990). Human speech perception pushes the auditory system to its limits of acoustic interpretation. Roederer (1995) has proposed that as human language evolved with the appearance of specialized cortical speech areas, "a drive emerged to train the acoustic sense in sophisticated sound pattern recognition" (p. 82) in preparation for language acquisition immediately upon birth. During intrauterine development, the acoustic sense of the fetus begins to perceive and store information from the sound environment. Most of these sounds involve communication with the mother. At birth the system changes to include active behavioral responses to acoustic communication. This enhanced system establishes the framework through which the neonate will learn which elements of his or her acoustic communication repertoire are effective in eliciting a desired emotional response from the mother, thereby creating a foundation for an emotional relationship with the mother. It also establishes the motivation to acquire language by attending to the mother's rhythmic and other musical sounds, listening, analyzing and storing those sounds, and generating similar sounds that lead to positive emotional feedback resulting from limbic reward dispensed by frontolimbic sections of the cortex. It is this same biological relationship between the brain's response to music/speech elements and its own capacity for reward and motivation that the music therapist activates and utilizes in the treatment process.

POSTNATAL AUDITORY PERCEPTION

During gestation, the human fetus receives musical and other sound stimuli from vibrations transmitted through amniotic fluid. There is ample evidence that the fetus reacts to these acoustic stimuli. Kovacevic (1993) reported on a study in which fetuses exhibited differential responses to different music. They were pacified by Mozart and Vivaldi, and disturbed by Beethoven and Brahms. To help understand *how* these stimuli and subsequent air transmitted vibrations can originate outside of the body and still have an effect on human brain functioning, this section is included to provide some background on the physics of sound energy, the anatomy and physiology of the human hearing mechanism, and the process of transduction as sound energy changes from vibration to auditory sensation.

At birth, the oscillating pressure waves that lead to auditory reception begin to be received through air instead of through amniotic fluid as was the case prenatally. The pinna, or outer ear, scatters some sounds and intensifies others such as those originating in front of the head (Hodges, 1980a). The external auditory *canal* channels pressure waves to the ear drum and, acting as a resonator, amplifies the pressure in sound waves in the range of 2000 to 5000 Hz by 5 to 10 db. The ear drum, or tympanic membrane, vibrates in response to the frequency and intensity of air pressure waves that disturb it.

The middle ear is next to respond to the oscillating waves of energy and includes three tiny bones known as ossicles which conduct the energy from the outer to the inner ear. The malleus extends from the inner surface of the tympanic membrane and its motion causes it to make contact with the incus. The incus in turn is connected to the stapes which is adjacent to the oval window. Because the ear drum is 15 to 30 times larger than the oval window and receives sound waves from relatively low resistant air instead of having to transmit it through relatively high resistant perilymph fluid, the ossicles work together to amplify the energy in the sound wave so that it is 25 to 30 times greater per unit of area on the oval window than it was on the ear drum (Hodges, 1980a).

The inner ear consists of the cochlea where the actual **transduction of sound energy** from oscillating pressure waves to electrochemical nerve impulses takes place. The perilymph conducts the waves to Reissner's membrane which forms the roof of the most important chamber of the cochlea, the cochlear duct, an area filled with endolymph between Reissner's membrane and the basilar membrane. Within the cochlear duct, the organ of Corti rests on the basilar membrane and contains Deiters' cells which support auditory hair cells tipped with cilia that extend upward through another membrane known as the reticular lamina. There the tallest cilia are imbedded in the tectorial membrane and all cilia of each hair cell are connected to adjacent cilia by a system of tip links and basal connections. When pressure in the endolymph causes the basilar membrane to move in opposition to the tectorial membrane, the resulting shearing action pulls the tips of each cilium toward the tallest cilia on each hair cell. The resulting tension on the tip links pulls open ion channels in the tip of each cilium allowing entry of potassium ions which causes depolarization of the action potential, increased release of neurotransmitter, and initiation of a nerve impulse in the associated cochlear nerve axon. This is how the transduction of pressure waves to neuroelectrical energy is accomplished (Carlson, 1992).

The afferent impulses that are created by the above process travel from the cochlea to bipolar neurons of the spiral ganglion. There the nerves carrying high frequency information from hair cells near the oval window, neurons from medial sections of the Basilar membrane, and low frequency impulses from hair cells near the apex of the cochlea, are arranged into one multifiber cable for transmission to the cochlear nuclei in the medulla. Although there is only one row of inner hair cells as compared to three rows of outer hair cells, each of about 95% of the incoming cochlear nerve axons brings impulses from a separate hair cell receptor in the inner row. The other 5% bring data from the outer rows at a ratio of ten hair cells to each cochlear nerve axon (Carlson, 1992). Higher frequencies are represented in the dorsal cochlear nucleus with lower frequencies in the ventral nucleus (Hodges, 1980a). Here also the nerves begin to interact to encode the spatial-temporal distribution of neural activity that is transmitted to the brain for cognition (Roederer, 1985).

Within the medulla, a majority of the fibers leaving each cochlear nucleus cross to the contralateral superior olivary complex. Other fibers go to the ipsilateral superior olivary complex, bilateral inferior colliculus in the midbrain, and reticular formation which plays a major role in arousal and attention. Because the superior olivary complexes receive information from both ears, they detect time and intensity differences, thereby playing a major role in determining sound localization. This information is sent to the lateral lemniscus which receives bilateral encoded data from the superior olivary complexes and sends it on to the inferior colliculus. At the level of the inferior colliculus, frequency, intensity, localization, and potential response to frequency changes are substantially completed and integrated. Reflex responses are available even though the evidence does not show conscious perception of sound at this stage for use by higher cortical centers (Roederer, 1995). The data is passed on to the medial geniculate body which receives bilateral stimuli to be shared with information from other sensory pathways and for transmission to the primary auditory cortex.

Until recently, it was believed that the actual sensation of sound did not occur until the pattern of impulses reached the primary auditory cortex in the temporal lobes. However, the latest literature shows that neither intensity nor frequency discrimination ability is impaired by total destruction of the human auditory cortex. Further research with animals has shown that without the auditory cortex, certain information about sound could not be determined such as temporal patterns, duration changes, localization, and changes in complex sounds. Destruction of auditory input to the medial geniculate body, however, did impair ability to detect sound intensity differences and frequency discrimination, thereby showing that a substantial amount of auditory perception ability is available at the level of the thalamus. Carlson has stated that "the perception of a simple stimulus can be accomplished by subcortical structures and does not require the presence of the cerebral cortex" (1992, p. 325).

The normal process of auditory transmission as described so far is automatic and involuntary until the sound reaches the cerebral cortex. How it is interpreted, recognized, stored, responded to, and later recalled depends upon the type and level of activity taking place in each person's brain at the time of stimulation. For example, if the person is asleep or attending intently to an alternate stimulus, processing may cease prior to the application of further strategies of cognition, resulting in minimal perception. However, if a music therapist has selected stimuli to which the patient can relate, and has presented them so as to facilitate maximum participation potential, it is quite likely that further brain activity will be stimulated. The following section describes brain activity involved in responding to auditory stimuli.

CEREBRAL PROCESSING OF AUDITORY STIMULI

The nature of brain activity in response to sensation has been the subject of much research and debate. Roederer (1985) is a proponent of the hololistic mode of storage and recall similar to the "hololistic representation" theory first proposed by Pribram (1971). According to this model, the brain developed a holographic-like system in which each and every point or feature of the object stimulus is projected throughout the entire domain of the image in order to facilitate immediate storage and recall. This can be interpreted to mean that as soon as the auditory cortex "hears" each sound, it sends all of the information about each sound (pitch, localization, timbre, duration, loudness, etc.) to all parts of the brain for response in accordance with each portion's primary function. Synaptic changes occur in neural circuitry that are sufficient to allow only a partial reintroduction of the original stimulus to "trigger the full pattern of neural activity specific to the entire original event" (Roederer, 1985, p. 76). This activity may include hearing, seeing, feeling, sensing, understanding, and ways of behaving in response.

The process described above takes place in areas for auditory and visual memory as well as in association areas of the brain such as the subjective evaluation systems in the frontal lobes. This pattern of continual synaptic formation and reformation in response to new stimuli can explain the often observed phenomenon of an otherwise nonverbal client or one with physical handicaps who suddenly demonstrates the ability to sing an entire previously learned song when only its title or a small number of notes is presented. The performance generally is accompanied by strong positive emotional reactions which are very motivating and reinforcing. Such reactions are due to concurrent activation of frontal lobe structures known as the orbitofrontal cortex and cingulate gyrus. The orbitofrontal cortex exchanges information with structures in the limbic system and receives information from other parts of the frontal lobes. It is responsible for translating judgments about social situations into actions and emotional responses. It communicates with the amygdala and with the cingulate gyrus which "appears to provide an interface between the decision-making processes of the frontal cortex, the emotional functions of the limbic system, and the brain mechanisms controlling movement" (Carlson, 1992, p. 331). The cingulate gyrus is involved in emotions and motivated behavior, and must be intact in order for the patient to talk or move. If damaged severely, death occurs.

Another structure in the limbic system that is extremely important in facilitating emotional responses to music and other stimuli is the amygdala. Located in the temporal lobe, the amygdala controls the integration of overt, autonomic, and hormonal reactions accompanying anger or fear. These conditioned emotional responses result in defensive, offensive, or escape behaviors in response to perceived objects or situations. The central nucleus of the amygdala sends axons to other brain structures including the hypothalamus, forebrain, medulla, and periaqueductal gray matter which is involved in pain and temperature control. The central nucleus also projects to other brain structures that are involved in reactions to aversive stimuli. Two of these regions are in the lower brain stem and help control autonomic nervous system functions. Another is a nucleus of the hypothalamus that is involved in the secretion of stress-related hormones. Extended stimulation of the central nucleus of the amygdala results in responses associated with long-term stress such as gastric ulcers.

Both pain and stress are important concerns that are addressed through musical applications in medical procedures. For example, Spintge and Droh (1987) have reported on their use of "anxiolytic" music to reduce anxiety, stress, and pain awareness in surgical, obstetric, and dental patients. Anxiolytic music is any music that has the effect of reducing stress response in cardiovascular and endocrinological systems. Consistent positive results were reported in their research concerning the use of music in medical procedures. They also made specific suggestions for selection and use of music in medicine.

A small but important structure that lies beneath the thalamus is the hypothalamus. Like the structures discussed above, musical stimuli have a strong effect upon its neurological firing patterns. The hypothalamus is extremely complex and controls the autonomic nervous system, the endocrine system, and organizes certain survival behavior such as anger and aggression, feeding and satiety, escape, drinking, sleeping, and reproductive reactions involved in mating. Musical stimuli reaching the hypothalamus can affect, for example, the cells that produce hormones which control the endocrine system. Stimulation of the hypothalamus and amygdala can also inhibit or elicit aggressive behaviors. The use of music in commercial establishments has provided long-term evidence of the effects of music on food intake, an activity that is largely controlled by the lateral hypothalamus (Carlson, 1992). Therapeutic applications of musical influences on hypothalamic parameters will be described in other chapters of this book.

From the above discussion, it should be clear that sensations such as sound, especially sounds such as music that can be emotionally stimulating through its form or its associative significance, can have a profound effect upon the processing patterns taking place in the patient's brain. Consequently, they also have a predictable and identifiable effect upon the observable behaviors resulting from musically stimulated brain activity. These behaviors are not, therefore, mystical or unexplainable nor are they due to unseen forces acting upon the human organism. They are the results of neurophysiological processing activated by musical stimulation.

DEVELOPMENT OF MUSICAL BEHAVIORS

As an individual grows, various characteristics, traits, and abilities develop as part of normal physical, psychological, emotional and social maturation. Among these is a wide range of musical abilities that are developed to some degree by every member of a society. The concept of musical ability is not limited in its application only to those individuals who aspire to become musicians in the sense of highly developed instrumental and/or vocal skills. Musical ability refers to a level of demonstrated or potential competence in any and all behavior in relation to music, both expressive and receptive. Each person who listens to, sings, plays, or responds to music develops some level of ability beginning at a very early age. It therefore becomes incumbent upon the music therapist to correctly assess the areas of experience and levels of ability exhibited in the musical behavior of each client.

Because brain functioning is the primary domain of music therapy intervention, it is essential that normal sequential development of human brain functioning, especially as it reflects cognitive development, be studied and targeted as a primary goal of music therapy. As Rogers (1990) has stated, "Jean Piaget is the best known of the cognitive theorists" (p. 7). In discussing Piagetian theory, Ostwald, (1990) proposed that musical ability appears to be associated with the preoperational child's development of stable concepts of melody, rhythm, harmony and form, particularly in forming principles of conservation regarding musical elements.

A large number of studies have been reported in the literature seeking to correlate the appearance of specific musical abilities with age and with the four main Piagetian developmental stages as indicated by use of their corresponding cognitive structures (Taylor, 1990). Familiarity with such correlations equips the music therapist to select musical tasks for therapeutic applications that will facilitate a balance between successful participation and challenge to reach higher levels of cognitive functioning. Continuous use of familiar, previously mastered types of musical tasks may eventually lead to boredom and apathy and may thereby cause progress to be slow. On the other hand, demands for levels of performance too far above the client's present cognitive and/or musical competence level may result in frustration and lack of participation. The proper way to plan a sequence of therapeutic interventions involving music would be to begin by utilizing the client's previously learned music skills, and gradually increase the levels of complexity in melodic, rhythmic, harmonic, or other musical characteristics as appropriate to the cognitive capacity to be expected of that individual.

Much of the research on development of musical behaviors has focused on the transition from preoperational logic to the stage of concrete operations as reflected in musical capabilities. Close examination of behavior at these stages shows that during the preoperational stage, the child does not exhibit role-taking capability, shows centration tendencies, and seeks cause-effect relationships. Most children do not appear capable of performing reversible mental operations on an altered stimulus, and therefore cannot demonstrate mental conservation under transformations of the stimulus. Their system of logic is dominated by intuitive reasoning. When operational logic is acquired at the onset of the stage of concrete operations, the child becomes capable of thinking independently from perception, decentering appears in perception of unified wholes, play is perceived as separate from reality, and the ability to mentally reverse an altered stimulus appears and provides the basis for conservation of volume, length, and time. Conservation, therefore, has become the mental capacity most studied by researchers in developmental musicology (Taylor, 1990).

Development of the cognitive structures referred to above is manifested in musical behavior by changes in responses to music as well as in the child's ability to be musically expressive. During the developmental period, musical behavior begins with sensorimotor responses such as heart rate dishabituation, feeding changes, and pitch matching, and progresses to a wide variety of both receptive and expressive behaviors during the preoperational stage. These include pitch and rhythm matching, vocal reproduction of melodic contour, spontaneous use of the descending minor third in interpersonal communication, maintenance of tonality, conservation of rhythm, direct intuition of duration, seriation, and conservation of velocity among five and six-year-olds, and recognition of sudden key changes during familiar tunes among seven-year-olds (Taylor, 1990).

The transition to concrete operations reflects improvement in ability to imitate tonal and rhythmic patterns, perception of durational changes, conservation of rhythm under melody deformation, conservation of tempo, and conservation of melody under rhythmic inversion and pitch transposition. Full acquisition of operational thought provides the cognitive structures needed to solidify these skills and to add conservation of meter and melodic phrases, and improved tonal memory, melodic perception and pitch discrimination. The move to the cognitive stage identified by Piaget as formal operations signals the earliest ability to use the operation known as "reciprocity" which allows subjects to reproduce inversions, retrograde and retrograde inversions (Taylor, 1990).

As music therapists apply musical procedures to patients in clinical situations, they must do so with full and constant awareness of the neurological impulse patterns that are being affected and the cognitive structures of which their patients' brains are capable. In the following section, the neurological basis of overt responses to music will be summarized.

MUSICALLY STIMULATED CHANGES IN BRAIN ACTIVITY

The scientific and related literature concerning musical effects on the brain is replete with reports of changes in brain activity. Investigations include study of sensory thresholds, cortical arousal levels, emotional behaviors, physical activity, electrochemical action potentials, levels of neurotransmitter release, and differential localization of neural activity under various stimulus conditions. These accounts are based on findings that explain the mechanisms underlying various processes that result in overt behavior. For example, there is a widely accepted view that rhythmic music stimulates movement of skeletal muscles, and that rhythm in music serves as a structure that is used by the brain for temporal organization of bodily movements. However, this belief does not include an understanding of how the brain accomplishes those tasks, how it organizes rapid digital fine motor movements in producing instrumental music, nor does it account for the changes in some autonomic responses in nonskeletal smooth muscle that accompany very rhythmic musical selections. In order to fully explain such responses to music, it must now be understood that movements especially of skeletal muscle result from musical auditory stimuli that disperse throughout the brain as generalized neuronal discharges. These impulses activate specific structures in the cerebellum, basal ganglia, frontal association cortex, primary motor cortex on the precentral gyrus, corticospinal pathway, corticobulbar pathway (controls movements of the face and tongue), and the rubrospinal tract which receives inputs in the red nucleus of the midbrain from the motor cortex and cerebellum. This tract then sends axons to synapse with neurons that control leg and arm muscles excluding the fingers. A more specific part of the process occurs when musically stimulated neural impulses reach the dentate nucleus in the cerebellum and it signals for movement to occur by triggering the discharge of preset neural patterns in the precentral motor cortex (Wilson, 1989).

The section above on cerebral processing of auditory stimuli describes the importance of the frontal association cortex in the processing of music and other auditory stimuli. When it is understood that the principal cortical input to the primary motor cortex is the frontal association cortex (Carlson, 1992), the connection between musical stimuli and rhythmically concurrent motor activity becomes clearer, and all musically generated overt responses that are mediated in the frontal lobes gain a much more consistent explanation.

The purpose of the present chapter is to demystify music as therapy by providing information needed to understand neurophysiological responses to music that take place in tangible and familiar structures of the human organism. An understanding of the Biomedical Theory of Music Therapy will provide both a theoretical framework within which to make informed decisions concerning selection and application of music in medicine as well as a philosophical foundation for further research.

In subsequent chapters, discussion of the biomedical model will continue with a presentation of the details of observed neurophysiological responses to music and their medical applications.

III

MUSICAL INFLUENCES ON CORTICAL PROCESSING

T he theory to be described herein is based upon a biological model of musical behavior. Its purpose is to provide a biomedical basis for interpreting receptive, expressive and physiological behavior of the human organism during musical participation. The basic premise for development of the theory is that:

> There are specific neurophysiological structures and processes that must be activated in order for certain behavioral responses to occur. Therefore, any occurrence of those behaviors in response to musical stimuli must result from the effects of music on those same neurophysiological structures and processes. Knowledge of those musical effects enables their use in medical and other therapeutic applications.

There are three fundamental assumptions forming a conceptual core around which the music therapist plans medical interventions utilizing musical influences. These are preliminary assumptions, not the theory itself.

a. Music affects each human being only because of the neurophysiological structures that each person possesses for receiving and responding to sound in the form of music.

b. Participation in music, whether receptive or expressive in nature, activates a wide range of specific and identifiable physiological and neuropsychological processes in the human body.

c. Musically activated neurophysiological responses are observable, measurable, and predictable, thus affording selection of music activities having predetermined positive effects on patients during medical procedures.

These three assumptions, as well as all applications of music as therapy, depend upon the same neurophysiological process: Once sensory stimuli in the form of musical sounds are received in the ear, they activate use of the auditory tract, enter the central nervous system via the medulla, and after passing through the thalamus, they are processed in the cerebral cortex. The brain develops its capacities in part because sense organs, such as the ears which accomplish transduction of sound waves, transmit the energy that generates brain development. The brain decodes and converts information and experience entering in the form of nerve impulses into sensations. It subsequently organizes and identifies stimuli, selects and directs reactions, stores information about the whole process, and recalls it as needed. By indulging in these operations, the brain develops its capacity for rationality, verbal and nonverbal communication, quantitative and qualitative computation, abstract thinking, and control of motor behavior.

This chapter will examine the medical implications of some of the principal issues related to the processing of music in the brain including hemispheric specialization, cortical arousal, cognition and disorders resulting in cognitive degeneration, and those biochemical substances that most influence the behaviors affected by music.

HEMISPHERIC PROCESSING OF MUSICAL BEHAVIOR

Professional literature containing investigations into the biology of music, psychology of music, psychomusicology, and music in medicine includes a substantial amount of work reflecting attempts to determine the cranial location of musical behavior, differences between the brains of musicians and nonmusicians, and hemispheric differences in the processing of musical behavior. Because those issues are so closely related to each other and to an understanding of the brain as the basis of therapeutic applications of music, some of the salient conclusions to be drawn from that work are summarized in this section. However, no attempt will be made to fully review that literature or its implications.

Evidence regarding cerebral localization of musical processing has been sought through studies of persons having abnormal brain phenomena resulting in seizures, hallucinations, aphasia or amusia, and through tests of normal subjects using dichotic listening, electrophysiological measures such as EEG, EKG, or EMG, and procedures designed to map brain physiology such as magnetic resonance imaging (MRI) and positron emission tomography (PET). Some investigators have focused on locating the sources of specific musical tasks while others have studied more comprehensive musical behaviors. The following listings attribute hemispheric locations for the processing of musical behaviors according to published literature reviews (Taylor, 1988, 1989; Bever, 1988):

Left hemisphere:
    Perception of rhythm
    Perception of musical information
    Identifying minute frequency changes of less than 30 cents
    Legato transients
    Melody recognition—among musicians
    Lyric performance during singing
    Sequential analytical aspects of music
    Receptive musical behavior
    General musical ability—among musicians

Right hemisphere:
    Processing of musical pitch
    Melody perception—nonmusicians
    Visual pattern recognition (necessary for reading music)
    Auditory pattern recognition (for tonal memory and timbre)
    Discriminating sound intensity changes
    Perception of musical chords
    Singing, specifically use of melody
    Attack transients
    Formulating a musical gestalt
    Expressive rhythmic and melodic behavior

Recent scientific studies have questioned the widely held view that music is processed in the right hemisphere of the brain. One area of focus has been hemispheric dominance rather than hemispheric specialization. Mazziotta et al. (1982) conducted a study that used PET scanning to show interhemispheric differences in metabolic activity in untrained and trained musicians during the Seashore tonal memory test. Results indicated that the untrained listener had the highest metabolic activity in the nondominant or right hemisphere while the trained musicians showed greater left brain metabolism, although the musical task was identical for all subjects. In reviewing this study, Walton et al. (1988) concluded that there was a distinctive pattern of brain activity associated with musical processing among trained musicians, and suggested that this may have been due to their use of a processing strategy analogous to that of language. Extensive research in the area of speech and language processing has disclosed that the language centers are found in the left hemisphere in approximately 97 percent of all cases (Taylor, 1989).

Some investigators have attempted to locate a music center in the brain more specific than an entire hemisphere. For example, within the Sylvian Fissure on the upper surface of the temporal lobe is an extension of Wernicke's area called the "planum temporale." Studies of planum asymmetry show that the planum is equal in size in about 24 percent of cases and larger on the right side in 11 percent. Roederer (1975) has suggested that a relatively large right planum temporale indicates greater inborn capacity for processing nonverbal sound, and could signal evidence of inborn musical ability. Another interhemispheric anatomical variation is in the polar area of the superior temporal region which is generally larger in the right hemisphere. Damage to this area often results in amusia or loss of musical abilities, thus prompting its implication as a prime source of musical capability in the human brain (Taylor, 1989).

The findings reported above certainly have not led to a conclusion that would identify one hemisphere or anatomical structure as the location for music in the human brain. Numerous investigators have concluded that there is no one area of the brain for music processing. In his presentation to the 1992 symposium on Music and the Brain, John Brust, M.D., reported that dichotic listening studies have claimed left ear advantage, right ear (left brain) advantage, no difference, musical aptitude difference, and age-related differences in perception of musical elements. He asserted that in studies of seizures, hallucinations, amusic patients, and experimental studies, the damage that destroys music cannot even be located. He disagreed with attempts by others to place musical processing in one part of the brain or in one hemisphere.

Manchester (1988) called attention to the complex interaction of physical and mental factors in producing music. He asserted that the brain "clearly" is the key element in musical performance. Based on research and professional literature by several physicians, he suggested that, "the brain probably does not have one area devoted to music activity; several sections of the brain probably play independent and interdependent roles in making music" (p. 148). Conclusions and opinions of this type can be found throughout the literature dealing with neurological processing of musical behavior, and they indirectly lend support to theories such as the holological processing model advanced by Pribram (1971) and Roederer (1985).

Other research by Morton et al. (1990), in which prior exposure to music improved memory and reduced distractibility, prompted the suggestion that the music may increase bilateral cerebral arousal levels by activating the music processing specialties of each hemisphere. The authors cited research indicating that right hemisphere arousal is superior for mediating bilateral arousal. It was therefore suggested that cognition could be improved through pre-task exposure to music in children who exhibit short-term memory difficulty in educational and therapeutic settings. The finding that the interhemispheric arousal effect extended beyond the presentation of the musical stimulus seemed to implicate experiential memory factors as a partial explanation for the inconsistent perceptual laterality effects often reported in dichotic studies. Experiential memory may interfere with performance *during* a dichotic listening or other task, whereas bilateral arousal perseveration may enhance task performance involving short-term memory skills *following* a musical stimulus. These findings and conclusions also may offer a viable explanation for popular claims of improved performance on intellectual tasks following exposure to the music of composers such as Mozart. A more thorough discussion of the effects of music on cortical arousal is included in the following section.

CORTICAL AROUSAL AND MUSIC

For many of the patients seen in medical and other settings, an important objective is to focus their attention upon stimuli that are based in external reality rather than on painful, anxiety-based or fantasized stimuli originating internally. Even the fear or expectation of pain may result in anxiety-related physiological reactions that can produce rejection of anesthesia prior to a procedure, unfavorable blood pressure or adrenocortical levels during the procedure, and extended discomfort during the recovery period afterward. Numerous studies, many of which will be cited in the following chapters, have shown that the negative effects of all these factors can be reversed or avoided by arousing the patient's awareness of musical stimuli under certain conditions. The neurophysiological basis of these effects lies in a sequential pattern of responses in the central nervous system, one of the most important of which is stimulation of the reticular formation, or RAS (Reticular Activating System).

The **Reticular Formation** consists of over ninety nuclei in a diffuse interconnected net of complex dendritic and axonal projections. It forms the core of the brain stem extending upward from the base of the medulla through the pons to the upper border of the midbrain. The RAS receives data from the ascending sensory pathways and projects axons to the cerebral cortex, thalamus, and spinal cord. It is active in regulating sleep, arousal and attention. Numerous studies have shown that stimulation of the reticular formation produced arousal. Sensory input, including musical stimulation, sends impulses through the RAS, thereby activating and sensitizing it to these incoming impulses prior to cortical awareness. The musically activated reticular formation then arouses the cerebral cortex by means of direct axonal connections and by other connections relayed through nuclei of the thalamus (Carlson, 1992).

Although it has been found that individual neurons of the reticular formation respond in relation to specific movements of the eyes, ears, face, head, body, and limbs, one nucleus, the locus coeruleus, does appear to have a profound effect on arousal through the widespread effects of its noradrenergic system which mediates catecholamine agonists that produce arousal and sleeplessness. These noradrenergic neurons fire at a high rate during periods of sensitivity to external stimuli (Carlson, 1992). It is, therefore, the activation of these noradrenergic neurons that is the true target of the therapist who seeks to arouse the patient to the awareness of external stimuli in the form of music.

As part of the arousal response pattern, the reticular formation plays a role in certain other processes such as muscle tonus, movement—particularly posture and locomotion, and some vital reflexes. Investigations by Sears established many years ago that music does produce changes in muscle tonus as measured by electromyograph recordings (1958), and that a musical selection does produce similar postural changes in subjects with regard to directional variation (1951). Although the neurophysiological basis for these findings could not be explained at that time, it now appears that musical stimuli, activating neural systems in the reticular formation, the dentate nucleus in the cerebellum, the frontal and primary motor cortex, and influencing in turn the rate of firing in the gamma motor neuron system, do have an effect upon muscle contraction resulting in measurable overt responses indicative of arousal.

Perhaps the most urgent need among medical patients for cortical arousal lies with the patient who is in coma. Because there are so many different levels of disability and ability among coma patients, there is no one single definition of coma that differentiates this condition from all other disabilities. Attempts have been made to create descriptive criteria to be used in classifying the several variants of coma observed in clinical practice. Examples of these are the Glasgow Coma Scale, the Munich Coma Scale, and the Rancho Los Amigos Levels of Cognitive Functioning Scale, which rate observed behaviors such as eye movements, reflexes, and responses to painful stimuli (Boyle, 1989). These instruments reflect the wide range of possible behaviors resulting from head injury, from a vegetative state of wakefulness without response to external stimuli to a level of consciousness in which purposeful, appropriate responses are exhibited. Having spent two days in coma some years ago, this writer can attest to one level of this condition as characterized by transient states of deep sleep alternating with periods of partial wakefulness in which some interpersonal responses are accomplished and resulting in temporary impairment in locomotion upon emergence into full consciousness.

Coma is most widely known as a result of severe head trauma such as a blow to the head. However, it may also result from excessive intake of barbiturates which depress brain activity by decreasing neuronal cell metabolism, thus producing difficulty in walking and talking, unconsciousness, coma, or even death. In addition, the most commonly used CNS depressant, ethyl alcohol in alcoholic beverages, progressively causes motor incoordination, unconsciousness, coma, and finally death when used in increasingly larger doses to reduce anxiety (Carlson, 1992).

Studies and reports throughout most of this century have concluded that consciousness is not necessary for music to beneficially affect large areas of the cerebrum (Taylor, 1981). Boyle (1989) reported cases in which contingent music was used to elicit behaviors from patients who were comatose or even in a vegetative state. Numerous accounts have appeared in medical literature and in the media illustrating the benefits of music in helping to bring patients out of the comatose state. In one example, Harvey (1992) reported a case that was related to him by a nurse which involved a patient in an Intensive Care Unit who was in coma. While making rounds, one of the nurses on the unit would pass the time by singing. After several days in a comatose state of unconsciousness, the patient regained consciousness and was eventually discharged. He later returned to the ICU area and sought out the nurse who sang. He thanked her for saving his life and reported that her singing helped him identify reality and was like a lighthouse that guided him back to life.

The issue for music therapy in medicine is to determine and understand exactly what the above patient's statements indicate about what was occurring on a neurological level in the comatose nervous system. It is now possible to describe with reasonable certainty what was actually taking place. As described above, musical sounds traveling as nerve impulses, even in the absence of consciousness, activate the auditory system and, through their inevitable passage through the RAS, create cortical arousal effects in the cerebrum that result in elevated skeletal muscle tonus. Kinesthetic feedback from the increased muscle tonus provides additional secondary cortical stimulation and supports the primary auditory input. These arousal effects generalize bilaterally in a hologic manner throughout all cerebral structures and are sustained due to continuous responding necessitated by the constantly changing auditory sensory field during musical stimulation, an advantage not afforded by occasional sounds in an ICU. Visual, olfactory and tactile stimuli are not available to serve similar arousal functions during coma due to the necessity for consciousness and motivated attending in order to receive sustained stimulation without habituation in the absence of change in these sensory fields. Intravenous feeding of coma patients in an ICU precludes use of gustatory sensory pathways. The auditory pathway, preferably carrying musical stimuli familiar to the patient, therefore becomes the primary means of achieving interhemispheric cortical arousal in the coma patient.

MUSIC AND COGNITION

Studies of cognition have included investigations of perception, identification, usage, storage, and recall of information, most of which originated as sensory stimulation. Operative during these activities are also emotional reactions, motivations, affective behaviors, and adaptive motor responses that contribute to the total effectiveness of cognitive processing by the human brain. These evocative aspects of behavior provide the interactive component necessary for the processing of information within a sociocultural context.

The objective of therapy is not to only help the patient attain an enlarged repertoire of coping behaviors, nor is it simply to provide additional knowledge. An important responsibility for any therapist is to assist patients in acquiring and utilizing the maximum capabilities of their brains in processing new information as it is received from the environment. Such processing includes accurate perception of present reality, sequencing and serial projecting of events, pattern recognition based on spatial, temporal, magnitude or other perceptual relationships, storage and recall using both short-term and long-term memory, and both the confidence and opportunity to effectively use these cognitive skills to process information in new situations.

Juan G. Roederer (1985), speaking to the International Symposium on Music in Medicine, said "Music (and art in general) lends itself well to a more comprehensive study that includes all evocative components in addition to the informative aspects of cognition" (p. 62). A common experience in all cultures is to learn specific information using a musical setting of that data as a mnemonic device. The "Alphabet Song" is an example that sets the letters of the alphabet sequentially to the tune of "Twinkle, Twinkle, Little Star." This technique of teaching and learning assists the brain in performing the memory components of cognition and provides important cues for recall or "recognition" of similarly presented stimuli on subsequent occasions. Although memory is a much more complex and important process than obtaining and filing units of information, it is the essential component in the process of transforming perception into learning. More about the neurophysiology of memory is included below.

Learning takes place when experience results in a useful change in behavior. Experiences are not, however, simply stored in ways similar to storage on an audio or video tape recorder. They change the way individuals perform cognitive skills and tasks by "physically changing the structure of the nervous system, altering neural circuits that participate in perceiving, performing, thinking, and planning" (Carlson, p. 404).

The function of learning is to develop patterns of behavior that allow the individual to adapt to the changing environment. The concept of "behavior" is generally interpreted to refer to an observable action or action pattern. This does not mean that learning takes place only in those portions of the brain that control movement, although motor learning is an important form of learning. The basic forms of learning also include perceptual learning, stimulus-response learning, and relational learning (Carlson, 1992). In perceptual learning, each sensory system of the brain develops the ability to recognize (identify and categorize) objects and situations by producing physical changes in the corresponding sensory association cortex. Learning to recognize music or other complex auditory stimuli therefore involves changes in the auditory association cortex located on the superior part of the temporal lobe. These changes allow the brain to store and recall stimulus patterns according to their unique properties. Tasks involving musical learning and recall should be asked of the patient when the goal is to activate, reactivate, or develop the capabilities of the temporal auditory association cortex as an aid to the enhancement of cognitive processing capability.

Stimulus-response learning involves acquisition of the ability to perform a particular behavior in the presence of a specific stimulus. It therefore requires creating connections between the neural circuits of perception and those that govern movement (Carlson, 1992). Hence, stimulus-response learning includes both relational learning when the individual relates the stimulus to a response, and motor learning when the neural circuits of movement are engaged in making the response.

Certain forms of music lend themselves very well to the integration of perceptual, stimulus-response, relational, and motor learning as well as to including both informative and affective aspects of cognition. Folk music, for example, by its very nature is an activity that traditionally requires and facilitates participation by including primarily songs that are simple, repetitive, functional, active, entertaining, informative, topically relevant to the vast majority of the members of a society, and which encourage individual and group creativity. Because of such characteristics, numerous forms of folk music are used in clinical settings to stimulate increased use of cognitive skills in the patient's brain.

A type of folk song that utilizes the characteristics and types of learning described above is one that includes pre-patterned folk dances or other actions as part of the normal experience of participation. These songs enhance cognitive processing by involving the brain in sequencing of information, short-term as well as long-term memory storage, and motor learning as individuals respond to auditory cues. Motor learning involves changes in neural circuits controlling movement, but is guided by sensory stimuli, making it a form of stimulus-response learning. Such songs may be as simple as "Itsy Bitsy Spider" or as complex as a square dance or action song. A song such as "She'll Be Comin' Round the Mountain" requires perception, use of short- and long-term memory, and sequencing of information both forward and backward.

Motor planning and learning also are practiced as cognitive skills when the actions are included with the activity.

Because of the integral importance of memory as a component of cognition, it deserves closer examination to determine how to use it as a therapeutic tool to enhance brain function. Singing songs such as those identified above requires and facilitates development of motor memory as an important cognitive capability. The tune, words, and actions must be processed in short-term memory and sent for storage in long-term memory, sometimes referred to as "working memory" and "reference memory" respectively. The cranial locations for these activities vary.

It is generally agreed that Broca's area, which lies just above the Sylvian fissure on the left side in most people, stores the sequences of muscular movements needed to articulate words in reference memory (Carlson). When the sound of a word to be spoken is received from Wernicke's area, which is found at the posterior end of the Sylvian fissure, Broca's area sends information from preprogrammed instructions to be carried out for the appropriate sequences of motor activities to the primary motor cortex. Therefore, when a patient is engaged in singing a song, the therapist is eliciting structured cerebral activation and purposeful use of the primary auditory cortex, Wernicke's area, Broca's area, bilateral frontal association cortex, and primary motor cortex. When the song also has accompanying actions or if the patient plays an instrument during the singing, the procedure also activates efferent pathways in the corticospinal pathway which has cell bodies in the primary motor cortex and ultimately controls the arms, hands, and fingers. Physical actions also activate bilateral use of the parietal lobe where spatial perception is handled. This information is forwarded to the frontal association cortex where it is used to plan locomotion and arm-hand movements, thereby resulting in active motor responses such as walking, clapping, waving, turning and/or playing an instrument, for example maracas, omnichord, or guitar. Because of the large amount of reality-based interhemispheric activity generated by such musical participation, it is believed that music activities that include motor responses are the most effective for decreasing the distance between a person's psychological environment and the physical and social environment of the real world.

All of the cerebral operations that contribute to the observed responses are worked out and placed in short-term memory for immediate use. They are then transferred to long-term memory for reference and recall at other times. Storage locations are in the frontal and posterior association areas such as the temporal association cortex located below the primary auditory cortex in the temporal lobes. Studies of these areas and the short term-long term memory transformation process in musicians have led to the recent discovery of neurophysiological events such as the P3 phenomenon. P3 is a positive brain wave that occurs approximately 300 milliseconds after the beginning of a task-related, infrequent, or surprising event.

Frisina, Walton, and Crummer (1988) have reported that a key function in cognitive processing during music is the transfer of "current sensory information from short-term memory to long-term memory, and conversely the comparison of long-term memories to incoming sensory information as it enters short-term memory" (p. 102). P3 is considered indicative of cognitive activity that occurs whenever it is necessary to update a model of the environment that is present in working memory by comparing it to incoming sensations or to data from reference memory. Like other phenomena to be discussed in the final section of this chapter, it is identified as "endogenous" because of its dependence primarily upon the internal mental state of the individual as opposed to being a reflex response to external events in the environment. It is "event-related" due to its occurrence in correlation with an internal or external event rather than occurring spontaneously or continuously as with some other brain wave activity.

It is possible that Piaget would have referred to the occurrence of P3 activity as indicative of disequilibration when the comparison of short-term, long-term, and incoming sensory information does not result in a close or exact match. In proposing the "Musical Enhancement of Cognitive Development" model of teaching music, Taylor (1990) urged introduction of separate musical elements at appropriate intervals to renew short-term disequilibration and foster new efforts toward accommodation.

Without labeling it as P3 activity, this same phenomenon may have been postulated when Mueller (1964) offered the following description of the effect of musical aesthetic stimulation on human psychological behavior:

> We now know that neural tissue is natively and persistently active, with its own characteristic rhythms or synchronies of firing sequences which can be recorded on the electroencephalograph.... These are large, slow waves similar to those of the adult during sleep. These rhythms, or patterns, which form a basic substratum of neural activity, are constantly broken into by sensory activity associated from outside stimuli. Instead of supporting rhythmic, long, slow waves already discharging themselves, such sensory activity has the opposite effect. It breaks up the established firing sequences and gradually changes them throughout life in the long, never-ending learning process. It is this give and take of the action patterns which makes for normal, coordinated, adaptive activities. (p. 8)

The P3 is considered to be the most well understood endogenous ERP, event-related potential, available for studies of cerebral cognition. Perhaps future research will yield positive findings of P3 hypoactivity among patients who exhibit cognitive impairments and for whom generous repetition of musical and other material is needed for even modest success in recall task performance. Clearly, the P3 ERP is one of the primary targets when music therapists and music educators share musical experiences with patients and students. The aim is for the participant to discover a relationship between current musical stimuli and similar experiences stored in long-term memory.

Cognitive impairment is the most consistent and identifiable character-istic of the group of conditions known as Developmental Disabilities. Disor-ders in cognitive ability may have toxic, metabolic, or traumatic origins, may be congenital, and may be hereditary. In the condition known as Down Syndrome, named for Dr. John Langdon Down who first described it in 1866, there is no inheritance of a faulty gene even though some mental retardation is a common feature. In over 75% of cases, the presence of a second 21st chromosome in the mother's ova results in three copies, rather than two, with addition of the father's 21st chromosome upon fertilization. The presence of this extra chro-mosome results in biochemical changes that impair normal fetal brain develop-ment (Carlson, 1992; Mader, 1995).

The brain is the primary focus with most developmentally disabled cli-ents seen for music therapy. Mental retardation, the most prominent group in this category, by definition involves subaverage intellectual functioning, mak-ing the brain always the focus of therapy. The etiology of mental retardation is varied, ranging from prenatal infection or drug or alcohol intoxication to an-oxia or trauma during prenatal, perinatal, or postnatal development. To com-bat anoxia, music is used at a hospital in Wisconsin to keep premature babies quiet and relaxed in order that oxygen levels in their blood will stay within the desired range rather than being used up by hyperactive physical and respiratory activity (kicking and screaming). They are often sick and have breathing prob-lems too severe to adequately replenish the blood oxygen supply to their brains.

Brain functioning may also be diminished due to metabolic disorders such as Phenylketonuria (PKU). With this disorder, an enzyme is lacking which normally would convert the amino acid phenylalanine into tyrosine, another amino acid. The excessive unconverted phenylalanine in the blood interferes with postnatal myelinization of nerves in the central nervous system. The re-sulting failure of normal brain development leads to severe mental retardation (Carlson, 1992).

When working with cognitively disabled or other brain damaged clients, it is helpful to conceptualize the brain in ways that will account for both ob-served and potential behaviors. The human brain has basically four types of areas, with separate classes of functions performed by brain tissue in each: Sen-sory—in which information is received from the external and internal environ-ments in the form of sensory stimuli; Association—in which information is organized, processed, stored, and decisions are made; Motor—which formu-lates and sends instructions to muscles for moving the body in relationship to the environment; and Emotional—structures that are specifically responsible for providing feelings and formulating emotional response behaviors.

Music therapy goals with developmentally disabled clients typically involve most or all of the above types of areas. Social goals, for example, are partially dependent upon the function of a portion of the limbic system known as the hippocampus (Thompson, 1967). Motor skills involve activity in the parietal areas. Communication skills such as auditory awareness, language, and nonverbal communication depend totally on the abilities of the sensory receptive, language specific, and motor areas of the brain. Academic skills such as attending, following directions, object classification, sequencing, seriation, concept formation, and short and long-term memory/recall place special emphasis on the association areas, but also involve activity in all four types of brain tissue. The same is true for self-help skills such as personal hygiene, decision making, goal setting, creativity, goal-directed behavior, and leisure skills.

Research findings regarding music therapy with developmentally disabled clients are many and they have demonstrated the effectiveness of music in enhancing cognitive processing. In one example of such findings, Dorow (1976) used televised general music lessons as reinforcement for correct math responses, and sought to determine whether mathematics achievement among educable mentally retarded subjects would improve. It was reported that the percentage of correct math responses increased from 65.5% during baseline to nearly 80% during the initial 2-week treatment period and to 82% in the second treatment period. In addition, correct responses on a Music Listening Skills Test showed a significant increase from pretest to posttest ($p < .005$). A more thorough examination of the biological mechanisms involved in reinforcement is contained in Chapter 6.

Developmentally disabled children are often seen by music therapists in school settings along with children having other exceptional education needs (EEN). Because these children's brains are developing, it is necessary to have an understanding of developmental findings as they relate to EEN children. Included among the children seen by music therapists in school systems are many who have learning disabilities. The U.S. National Joint Commission on learning disabilities defined L.D. in 1981 as having "significant difficulties in acquisition and use of listening, speaking, writing, reasoning, or mathematical abilities... and presumed to be due to central nervous system dysfunction." Clearly the brain is the focus of treatment when working with these children.

Another type of disability that is characterized by cognitive impairment is autism. Autistic behavior reflects a profound failure to develop social relationships or normal communication skills, and a continuing state of hypoactivity (Denkla, 1990). If verbal behavior is exhibited, it may lack prosody which is the melody, rhythm and accentuation of normal speech. Magnetic resonance image (MRI) diagnostics reveal that certain parts of the cerebellum are lacking, in particular the cerebellar vermis appears to be abnormal. Dr. Temple Grandon, who was herself autistic while growing up, has confirmed the existence of a decreased vermis area of the cerebellum in autistic children, resulting in extended perseveration behaviors in the autistic brain. This condition limits the availability of neural signals necessary for cortical arousal, thereby resulting in underactivation of the cerebral cortex which, in all other measurements except the limbic system, appears normal. However, autistic patients do learn to participate in music, even to the point of playing instruments. They respond actively during musical activities and will initiate such activity if given the materials and opportunity. Cortical arousal, therefore, appears positive under musical stimulation.

In work intended to describe the therapeutic effects of music on autistic and schizophrenic children, Hudson (1973) described the autistic ego as not having developed, and the schizophrenic child as having developed with a distorted ego. He then characterized rhythm in music as a language having physiological appeal in ego restructuring with autistic and schizophrenic children. The neurophysiological mechanism for this effect was addressed in J. Roederer's discussion of the psychophysics of music when he theorized that "The propagation through cerebral tissue of a cyclically changing flux of neural signals triggered by rhythmic sound patterns may... enter into resonance with the natural clocks of the brain that control body functions and behavioral response" (1975, p. 165).

Numerous writers have reported success in using musical interventions with autistic patients (Saperston, 1973; Mahlberg, 1973). Jacobs (1987) reported a study in which an autistic child developed increased socialization, compliance, attention to musical activities, ability to sing a melody, match pitch, and exhibit remarkable memory for melodies and words. Alvin and Warwick (1991) reported that their use of music therapy with autistic children resulted in development of consciousness, self-expression, and creativity. Perhaps the increased cortical arousal afforded by musical audiation allows the autistic person to attend to a musical stimulus in contrast to the otherwise nonaroused cortical state during the absence of music.

What appears to be a possible "Theory of Autism" emerges to explain its etiology in terms of inhibition of cortical arousal. Specifically, lack of ability to attend to environmental stimuli may be a result of inhibited cortical arousal due to congenital deformity of cerebellar structures and the accompanying inadequate development of the neural pathways that would carry impulses from the reticular activating system to the dentate nucleus of the cerebellum for passage on to the thalamus, which in turn would alert the cortex to prepare to respond to certain stimuli. Without the ability to complete this arousal function, the underdeveloped nervous system would leave the cerebral cortex focused upon whatever stimulus or thought it was occupied with before the new information arrived. New stimuli would be analogous to a guest arriving at a party without being announced to the previously assembled guests. Existing conversational topics, associations, and interactions would continue with little or no notice of the new arrival until that newcomer had devoted time and effort to circulating sufficiently to accomplish self-announcement.

Other disorders resulting in cognitive impairment are schizophrenia and Alzheimer's Disease. Because a more thorough examination of the biomedical effects of music on schizophrenia is included in Chapter 8, this section will focus on dementia of the Alzheimer's type (DAT).

The term "dementia" refers to impairment in intellectual ability due to organic brain disorder (Carlson, 1992). Alzheimer's disease is an irreversible progressive brain disease affecting approximately 5 percent of the population above the age of sixty-five. Confusion in processing incoming sensory information, difficulty with common tasks, and memory deficits especially of recent events characterize this disorder. Although its actual cause is unknown, it has been found that neurons that produce acetylcholine are among the first to degenerate, thereby resulting in the early memory loss characteristic of the beginning stages of the disease. It has also been hypothesized that a faulty gene accounts for the excessive production of amyloid, a protein that may be a contributing factor in the disease. The nerve cells of the cortex continue to degenerate until the brain can no longer perform the cognitive tasks necessary for survival or regulate the body's metabolic equilibrium.

The biomedical implications of music as it affects the brain of the Alzheimer's patient have been discussed by Walton, et al. (1988). They report direct evidence indicating that the disease attacks the hippocampal formation of the temporal lobe. The hippocampus is an essential component in human memory and a primary neural generator of the P3 action potential. Numerous studies, some of which are described below, have provided conclusive evidence that structured music therapy is effective in increasing both socialization and memory skills of DAT patients. During musical interventions, DAT patients exhibit strong reactions and focused attention, even with significant progression of the disease. These reactions include bodily movements, dancing along with the musical stimulus, singing, increased socialization, decreased agitation, and increased enjoyment. "Very few other activities do this" (p. 135). It was suggested that when perceiving and responding to music, Alzheimer's patients may use unique or alternate neural processes for cognition and memory.

Recent work by music therapists tends to support the hypothesis that brain stimulation through music may prompt the use of alternative processing circuits in the brain of the Alzheimer's patient. Silber and Hes (1995) draw this exact conclusion in suggesting that, "Creative [song] writing appears to utilize an intact portion of the brain and thus partially compensates for the affected areas" (p. 33). They reported that songwriting provided an opportunity to counteract some of the negative emotional, social, and cognitive aspects of the disease. The patients socialized, interacted, and communicated while writing, correcting, improving, and adding to what had been written. Through musical intervention, Alzheimer's patients partially and temporarily overcame apparent cognitive, memory, and language deficits. In another study by Pollack and Namazi (1992), Alzheimer's patients exhibited significant increases in direct verbal, direct nonverbal, and indirect social behavior. Of all social behaviors recorded, 62% occurred after music. Cooperation and attentiveness was exhibited during music sessions. Only four of the eight subjects exhibited instances of distraction or apathy in only seven of 48 sessions. Subjects participated, displayed physical energy, positive affect, increased and more fluent verbalization, pleasure, and initiative by leading singing, dancing, or by playing piano. Improvised harmonic, melodic, rhythmic, and dance movements revealed musical skills preserved from early years of life. Increases in nonverbal, verbal, indirect interaction, and motor activity accompanied by decreases in active sensory and passive behavior prompted the authors to suggest that subjects may have been predisposed to interact socially after music due to the state of increased alertness generated by the music. This observation reflects and reinforces the need for research and application of findings reported above regarding enhanced cognitive capability after music due to musically stimulated cortical arousal.

Other work reported by Prickett & Moore (1991) demonstrated the effectiveness of using long-familiar songs to stimulate successful use of memory skills in patients diagnosed with probable Alzheimer's disease. Patients exhibited better recall for words of songs than for spoken words or spoken information. Even when words could not be remembered, patients attempted to sing, hum, or keep time with the singing of the therapist. With consistent practice, some patients showed the capability for learning new song material even in the absence of ability to learn or recall new spoken material. Perhaps a general conclusion concerning observed effects of music on brain functioning in Alzheimer's patients is best summarized in a statement by Walton, et al. (1988) who noted that, "In the face of their impaired cognitive abilities the responsiveness to music is quite remarkable" (p. 135).

BIOCHEMICAL RESPONDENTS

Because of the importance of certain biochemical substances in facilitating specific functions, it is important for the reader to be familiar with each substance by name, by category, and by its musically stimulated influence on normal or abnormal brain functioning. Carlson (1992) has provided an excellent review of these substances. Reference will be made to the role of these substances in subsequent chapters.

When musical impulses are transmitted throughout the brain in a holological fashion, they activate the release of transmitter substances with each synaptic leap that they accomplish. These substances are known as neurotransmitters and, along with neuromodulators, hormones, and pheromones, control the behavior of individual cells, organ systems, or the entire organism. In order for neurotransmitters to have an effect when released by a neuron, they must be detected by protein molecule receptors in the membrane of a nearby cell. Neuromodulators are released similarly but in larger amounts to travel farther than the next adjacent neuron. They modulate the activity of many neurons in a particular area of the brain. Pheromones are released into the environment through sweat, urine, or specialized glands. Their odor affects the reproductive physiology of other animals of the same species. (Carlson, 1992).

Hormones are released by the endocrine glands and travel throughout the body via the blood stream. They influence behavior by stimulating receptors in certain cells in the brain, thereby changing the activity level of those neurons. The two types of hormones are peptides and steroids and they are detected by two separate types of receptors. Steroids travel to cell nuclei and eventually alter their protein production. Peptides are chains of amino acids and are particularly important in producing certain responses that form clinical objectives when using a musical intervention. For example, some peptides appear to serve as neurotransmitters whereas others function as neuromodulators and seem to have an effect on sensitivity to pain, a primary clinical objective of music therapy in nearly all general hospital applications. An important neuromodulator that is produced in the brain is a category of peptides called "endogenous opioids" also known as "endogenous morphines," or "endorphins" which reduce pain awareness by stimulating specialized receptors in the brain. These peptides also appear to regulate certain defensive behaviors as well as eating and drinking, the ultimate concern in work with eating disorders clients. A transmitter substance known as neuropeptide Y also has been found to be an extremely powerful stimulant for eating behavior.

Neurotransmitters are extremely important to musical stimuli in helping them to accomplish their therapeutic task of influencing brain function. Perhaps the most widely known neurotransmitter is acetylcholine (ACh) because it is released at synapses on skeletal muscles making it easily accessible for research measurements. ACh receptors on skeletal muscle produce depolarizations and thereby enhance excitation of the muscle fiber. On cardiac muscle, ACh produces hyperpolarization which inhibits the muscle potential. ACh also is found in the brain where it is involved in learning, memory, and sleep behavior. It is believed by some investigators that degeneration of acetylcholinergic neurons is responsible for short-term memory loss in Alzheimer's disease.

The subcategory of monoamines known as catecholamines includes epinephrine, norepinephrine, and dopamine, all of which play important roles in musically influenced behaviors. Epinephrine, also called adrenaline, is secreted by the adrenal medulla. Norepinephrine (NE) is synonymous with noradrenalin. Its neurons in the brain help control alertness and wakefulness, and it normally has an excitatory effect on its target organs in the sympathetic nervous system. Dopamine (DA) may have either an excitatory or inhibitory effect on postsynaptic potentials. As a neurotransmitter, it has been associated with many functions that comprise goals and objectives in music therapy such as movement, attention, learning, and addictions. It also has been implicated as an agent in schizophrenia since it was discovered that drugs which inhibit dopaminergic neurons alleviate schizophrenic symptoms. Breakdown of DA produces melanin, the substance that colors skin, and which normally causes a portion of the midbrain to be stained black. A fourth monoamine, serotonin (5-HT) produces inhibitory postsynaptic potentials and plays a role in mood (sedation-relaxation), control of eating, sleep, arousal, and in pain regulation.

The final group of neurotransmitters is the amino acid group. These are the most common transmitter substances in the central nervous system. Instead of being synthesized within neurons as are ACh and the catecholamine monoamines, amino acids are secreted directly as transmitter substances. One of their effects is to raise or lower thresholds for excitation of action potentials, a common objective of music therapy especially in certain medical applications where sensory thresholds are of foremost importance.

While this section has included only an introductory summary of certain endogenous biochemical substances, it is intended only to familiarize the reader with the existence and importance of the substances described. Additional references, often with more specific explanations, will be made to these substances in the following chapters.

IV

THE BIOMEDICAL
THEORY OF
MUSIC THERAPY AND
PAIN MANAGEMENT

The information, assumptions, findings, and processes stated in the three preceding chapters along with data to be presented in subsequent sections lead to one generalized conclusion which can be stated as the basic Biomedical Theory of Music Therapy:

> Music influences human behavior by affecting the brain and subsequently other bodily structures in ways that are observable, identifiable, measurable, and predictable, thereby providing the necessary foundation for its use in treatment procedures.

Upon reviewing the growing body of literature describing research and medical uses of music, certain recurring themes tend to appear with sufficient regularity to allow categorization of musical influences on biological processes that are important to medical and related procedures. Four hypotheses have been formed which are described separately in this and the following three chapters. The descriptions include supporting citations from clinical reports and published research.

The first of the four hypotheses, which together form the Biomedical Theory of Music Therapy, deals with pain:

> Hypothesis 1: Because all sound stimuli are accessed by all parts of the brain, sound as music affects pain perception through its direct effect on the ability of the somatosensory cortex to receive pain sensations ascending through the spinothalamic tract following reception by sensors in the peripheral nervous system.

The applicability of this principle is reflected in the work of numerous investigators who have reported uses of music which resulted in decreased overt pain responses, reduced pain sensations as indicated in patient reports of music's analgesic effects, and decreased amounts of anesthetic or analgesic medication needed both during and following surgical and obstetrical procedures. What causes these effects? Previous descriptions have relied on a distraction hypothesis, which explains music as a distraction that draws attention away from awareness of pain and refocuses it on musical stimuli (Mandel, 1988; Clark, et al., 1981; Hanser et al., 1983).

Another more biologically based explanation has enlisted the arousal functions of the reticular activating system by claiming that receptive musical audiation depresses awareness of pain indirectly by causing the reticular activating system to arouse the brain to focus on music instead of on pain sensations (Cook, 1981). However, it has not been determined why music would be chosen over the many other stimuli available to the RAS at any given time. Still, the presence of music has been determined to produce analgesia—a reduction in sensitivity to pain. Michel and Chesky (1996), in reporting conclusions drawn from their review of music and pain studies, recommended to a 1994 International MusicMedicine Symposium that investigators become more rigorous in establishing a scientific rationale for applying music therapy in pain relief. In the following section, this effect will be explained in terms of neuro-physiological processes and biochemical reactions.

PAIN PERCEPTION AND MUSICAL INFLUENCE

Because pain abatement is perhaps the most widespread use of the analgesic effect of music in physical medicine, the explanation of the mechanism for musical analgesics is one of the most important in biomedical theory. It is also one of the most compelling and begins with an identification of the receptors for pain sensation that lie in the peripheral nervous system.

PAIN RECEPTORS

Pain sensation is one type of somatosensory stimulus that is detected by both cutaneous and organic (internal) sensors. Pain generally results from events that cause damage to skin and other kinds of tissue. Hence, it has a positive role in notifying the brain that something has gone wrong in an area of the body.

Among their many receptors, both hairy skin and hairless (glabrous) skin have free nerve endings just below the surface which detect damage to cells and transmit pain messages to the central nervous system. Free nerve endings are the receptors for painful stimuli and are found also in membranes covering muscles, in tissue lining the joints, and in the body of muscles. An injury results in rupture of a capillary and tissue cells, thereby stimulating mast cells to release bradykinin, a molecule that causes the free nerve endings to fire sending pain impulses via peripheral nerves toward the central nervous system. Axons carrying pain impulses enter the central nervous system through dorsal root ganglia in the spinal cord where they form synapses with other neurons. The axons from this next relay of neurons cross to the contralateral side of the spinal cord and ascend to the ventral posterior nuclei of the thalamus which, in turn, project axons to the primary somatosensory cortex located behind the central sulcus in the human brain (Carlson, 1992; Mader, 1995).

MUSIC AND PAIN PERCEPTION

Pain perception is not an inevitable result of stimulation of pain receptors. Rather, "it is a complex phenomenon that can be modified by experience and the immediate environment" (Carlson, p. 201). It is generally believed among investigators that peptide neurotransmitters are active in the control of sensitivity to pain. Serotonin, a monoamine transmitter, is released at most synapses and participates in the regulation of pain by producing inhibitory postsynaptic potentials.

Since the early 1970s, investigators have known that pain perception can be modified by a variety of environmental stimuli. Volumes of reports from medical and dental uses of music have established that music is one of the more reliable of these environmental stimuli. By activating analgesia-producing neural circuits, these stimuli induce the release of endogenous opiates (explained below) which then stimulate opiate receptors on neurons in the periaqueductal gray matter of the thalamus. These thalamic neurons may also be activated directly through synaptic connections with various neural pathways. Connections from the periaqueductal gray matter activate neurons located in the nucleus raphe magnus of the medulla. These neurons then send axons to the gray matter of the dorsal horn of the spinal cord where their function is to inhibit the activity of neurons bringing pain information into the CNS for transmission to the brain.

Endogenous opiates, similar to opiate drugs such as opium, morphine, heroin, codeine, and methadone, produce analgesia (not anaesthesia because the patient remains conscious) by stimulating specialized receptors in the brain. These receptors are opiate receptors and their normal function is to monitor the presence of endogenous opioids such as dopamine or norepinephrine. Opioids bond with opioid receptors—particularly in the gray matter of the midbrain to 1) produce analgesia and 2) stimulate the neuronal system involved in reinforcement. Any stimulus or sensation, such as music, which can stimulate or increase endogenous opioid (endogenous morphine or endorphin) production will produce an analgesic effect by activating opioid receptors in the periaqueductal gray matter of the midbrain. There is ample literature affirming that music has been found to enhance endorphin production (Scarantino, 1987). There are also many studies reporting success in applying music for analgesia.

ANALGESIC MUSIC IN SURGERY

The effects of music in the process of surgery are often vital in increasing the chances of survival for surgical patients. As Spintge (1989) has explained, patients undergoing surgery often experience a reduction in general immune response, impaired resistance to infectious diseases, unsatisfactory healing of wounds, increased basal metabolic rate and heightened risk of cardiac infarction, heart attacks, cardiovascular collapse and death. Under these conditions, the demand for analgesics, sedatives and anesthetics increases. The author observed that the emotional state of the patient is responsible for the amount of postoperative pain sensation, which has a direct effect upon patient compliance and cooperation during rehabilitation. Shapiro and Cohen (1983) also observed that a neurophysiological response to a specific painful stimulus varies according to individual personality and pain threshold. They also concluded that anxiety associated with a painful experience promotes stress, fear and panic which intensifies a person's reaction to pain.

Music has been found beneficial during preparation for surgery, in the operating room, and during recovery. Among the factors that have been found to decrease in relation to the use of music are fear, anxiety, pain awareness, use of anesthetic agents, rejection of anesthesia, surgical team tensions, mortality rates, recovery periods, hospital stays, postoperative medications, and medical costs. Before reviewing published reports of such values derived from music in the surgical suite, it is important to understand the anesthesiologist's responsibility in maintaining the delicate balance between life and death in the operating room and how the introduction of music is helping to manage that responsibility.

ANESTHESIOLOGY

One of the major applications of music during a surgical procedure is to assist in pain abatement. However, the history of attempts to avoid pain during surgery reveals the use of much more intrusive and dangerous techniques. Centuries ago, a person was rendered unconscious to avoid pain by striking hard a wooden bowl placed on the individual's head, strangling until the person passed out, or administering large quantities of alcohol or opiates. No procedure was reliable and the amounts of alcohol or opiates needed were dangerously close to the amounts that would cause death. Also, these drugs do not suppress the brain's ability to respond to bodily injury with "surgical shock" which results in intense activity of the parasympathetic nervous system that dilates blood vessels and greatly reduces blood pressure, often leading to fatal heart failure. In the mid-nineteenth century, experimentation with the newly discovered anesthetics ether and nitrous oxide led to their use in dentistry and surgery because they could produce both unconsciousness and pain desensitization. While ether was preferred due to the greater stability of its effects and to its ability to produce deep prolonged anesthesia, it is extremely flammable and has been replaced by more recently discovered nonflammable anesthetics that also reduce the occurrence of surgical shock (Carlson, 1992).

PAIN AND ANXIETY REDUCTION WITH MUSIC

Spintge (1989) reported on an extensive study using pre- and postoperative standardized questionnaires to determine the effectiveness of perioperative applications of music. The music was selected in advance by the patient and was administered using earphones and music from compact disc players. The earphones were given to each patient in the preoperative waiting room and worn until the patient was asleep when general anesthesia was used. During an operation using local or regional anesthesia, the patient was able to listen to the music during the entire procedure. Among the reported results were a rise in the pain threshold, increased pain tolerance, and an approximate 50% reduction in the usual dosage of sedative and analgesic drugs.

Semelka (1983) reported numerous general hospital uses of music in anesthesiological practice. Among these was a report of an older lady who enjoyed hearing music during spinal anesthesia. One young man who had become a paraplegic as a result of an automobile accident, claimed to be resistant to anesthesia and therefore felt pain regardless of the medications. He agreed to have music played during preoperative administration of the anesthetic and he subsequently exhibited no pain awareness during removal of a skin ulcer.

The surgical team discontinued the narcotics, but continued the operation with music. The patient did not complain of pain until three days after the operation had been completed.

In a study of forty-eight male patients between the ages of 40 and 90, the patients underwent prostate or bladder surgery with either a standard i.v. dose of the anesthetic Diazepam as the operation began or music through head-phones throughout the operation. Music was generally slow in tempo with restrained dynamics, soft timbres, small intervals, nonsyncopated rhythm, and uniform ascending and descending melodic contour. The surgical team con-cluded that anxiety was reduced to a level equal to that of an additional dose of a tranquilizer without undesirable side effects, and that music was a technically simple and effective method that could be used with "good success" especially in conjunction with regional anesthesia (Sehhati-Chafai & Kau, 1985).

Susan Mandel (1988), a Registered Music Therapist, has reported on the planned use of music for postoperative pain abatement during her own spinal surgery experience. Music that had been pre-selected included ballads (songs with lyrics that told a story), music with a strong beat, and music that carried positive emotional associations with people or experiences. Although the writer had undergone two prior spinal operations with a "long and difficult" first night following each one, she reported no memory of postsurgical pain while regaining consciousness from the anesthetic following the third procedure. She also reported that the use of taped music during the administering of pain medication resulted in decreased need for the medication and in her ability to be discharged two days earlier than expected.

At the Seventh World Congress of Music Therapy in 1993, Sabina Puppo, then Secretary of the Governing Board of the Music Therapy Founda-tion in Buenos Aires, Argentina, provided a synopsis of the objectives and val-ues to be gained from music in the surgical process. After observing that music therapy has made important advances in surgical applications, she proposed that music be used in the preoperative stage to demystify the operation, balance internal rhythm, encourage relaxation and body awareness, raise the pain threshold, diminish anxiety levels, and prepare the patient for the anesthetic and operation. Immediately prior to surgery, music was proposed as a means of diminishing muscular tension and regulating blood pressure, body tempera-ture and pulse in order to allow the maximum effect of the anesthetic and use the least amount of it as possible. During surgery, the music would have an enabling effect on the patient under anesthesia by masking the sounds of sur-gical team conversations and other operating room noises. In the postoperative phase, it was proposed that the music be administered to facilitate the general recovery process through its positive effects on post-shock reactions and ho-meostatic maintenance.

At this Seventh World Congress, Alain Carre of Rennes, France, in the abstract of his presentation reported the results of a recent research project conducted in the Children's Surgery Service of Rennes Regional Hospital Centre. There was a high incidence of satisfaction with 90% of the patients who had been subjected to music reporting feeling "happy." The investigators also noted an approximate 32% decrease in the amount of anesthetic substances used during the operations. Music also helped reduce anxiety prior to the operations. Specific analgesic effects were noted during the postoperative period with less awareness of pain upon awakening from the anesthesia, and in some cases, total absence of pain.

In addition to the positive effects of music on pain abatement for the patient, the effects of music on the surgical staff have been noted. Puppo, whose work is mentioned above, has observed that music helps the anesthetist and other surgical staff members work in a relaxed atmosphere. Cook (1981) also has reported the work of investigators who indicated that the professional staff may benefit from the warmer and more pleasant atmosphere, closer harmony within the team due to decreased tension and fatigue, rhythmic stimulation of coordinated movements, and improved staff morale and efficiency through reduction of monotony during preparation and cleanup. Numerous writers have asserted that a patient with reduced pain awareness and decreased anxiety presents far fewer problems for the anesthetist and surgical team than one whose anxiety level and fear of pain are elevated.

MUSIC FOR PAIN MANAGEMENT IN CHILDBIRTH

The general hospital area most similar to the operating room is the conventional obstetrical unit. The evolution of the modern delivery room began centuries ago when the pain of childbirth was accepted as a normal part of the experience. Development of modern medicine brought ways of decreasing associated pain and mortality risks. These included aseptic techniques, general, regional and local anesthesia, and other methods that transformed the childbirth experience into a surgical procedure performed in the hospital (Clark et al., 1981). Consequently, the role of the mother became more passive.

In more recent decades, efforts have been made to return to the mother control of her own fear, tension and pain. There is greater recognition of psychological variables in pain mediation such as negative expectations of pain, anxiety which results in decreased thresholds for perception of stimuli, and special symbolic meaning that may be attached to pain perception. Clark, McCorkle, and Williams (1981) reported on a study which found that both pain and enjoyment were distinct dimensions of the childbirth experience.

In their own study, these investigators used questionnaires to measure subjective perceptions of amount of support received from significant others and from medical staff, anxiety level during childbirth, level of pain perception during delivery, length of labor, amount of pleasure or enjoyment, retrospective perception of helpfulness of prenatal childbirth classes, and helpfulness, frequency and length of practice sessions for Lamaze techniques. The 13 experimental subjects were scheduled for six individual music therapy training sessions and were required to attend at least four in order to be included in the sample. These sessions consisted of relaxation training, familiarization with the music therapy techniques to be used, and selection of music to be used at the time of delivery. Upon entry of each subject into the labor and delivery unit, the music therapist was notified. Music therapy was begun as soon as the therapist arrived and continued until the patient left the delivery room. Control group subjects experienced regular hospital labor and delivery routine.

Statistical analysis of the results revealed that respondents who had been participants in the music therapy procedure experienced significantly greater positive perceptions of the childbirth experience, more support from medical staff, and greater length of Lamaze home practice time than control subjects. The greatest differences were in perceived support from significant others, reported anxiety, helpfulness of Lamaze techniques, and levels of pain or discomfort. Correlation analysis revealed that frequency and length of music therapy home practice was a better predictor of success in the childbirth experience.

In a study by Hanser, Larson, & O'Connell (1983), seven expectant mothers and their coaches were trained in a six-week course taught by a certified childbirth educator. Sessions consisted of instruction in breathing patterns, relaxation, positioning and muscular control, focusing attention away from contractions, and offers of supervised practice sessions. Six women also experienced two separate individual music therapy sessions with each of two music therapists. These sessions used background music to cue rhythmic breathing, assist in relaxation, and focus attention on the music instead of on discomfort and hospital noises. The purpose of the study was to determine the effect of music on responses to pain during labor. Responses observed and rated consisted of behaviors such as flexed foot, eyes squeezed shut, hands clutching bed, position changes, irregular breathing, verbalizations, and coughs. Observations were made during ten contractions with music, alternating with five contractions without music. Musical selections were preselected by the mother and coach. Statistical analysis of the results showed that pain responses were significantly higher during no-music conditions than during music conditions. Verbalized pain responses also were significantly higher during no-music conditions. All of the mothers in the experiment emitted fewer pain responses during music than during no background music in the same setting.

The results reported above are supported by research from Germany in which a group of physicians (Halpaap et al., 1985) studied two hundred women for their subjective and objective reactions to childbirth. It was reported that over 80% of those who elected to have music before and during delivery experienced definite relief from pain and anxiety, although they were not made aware that the music was a research variable.

Results similar to those reported in this section have been recorded in numerous studies of the effectiveness of music for pain abatement, making obstetrics one of the clearest demonstrations of the validity of Hypothesis 1 in the Biomedical Theory of Music Therapy. Further data regarding the effectiveness of music in controlling anxiety and tension in both mother and baby during the delivery and postpartum periods is contained in Chapter 8.

PAIN MANAGEMENT WITH BURN PATIENTS

A medical-surgical hospital can be a place that offers hope and rehabilitation for patients who come with a wide variety of illnesses, injuries and disabilities. Perhaps none is more difficult for patient, staff, and family to manage than the type of injuries found in the burn unit. These patients are generally thought of as being among the most severely ill in the hospital (Christenberry, 1979). There is often a combination of emotional, psychological, and physical damage to individual patients that must be handled with great care and skill. Hospital stays continue for weeks or months, and it is not uncommon for a patient to remain hospitalized for over a year.

THE BURN UNIT

In order to apply music as therapy in the milieu of the burn center, it is necessary to understand the importance of what this modality brings to the treatment team as well as the implications of expected protocol and procedure that are in place to protect the patient and promote healing as effectively as possible. It should be noted that when a burn injury occurs, some or all of the protective qualities of human skin—waterproof, shock resistant, heat resistant, sensitive to touch, impermeable to bacteria, self-repairing—are lost. In addition, there may be swelling, damage to lungs with associated respiratory impairment, and injury to muscles and bones that seriously interferes with mobility and function. Intravenous fluid therapy and its accompanying equipment usually are engaged to replace essential fluids and their nutrients. The burn center and its treatment paraphernalia, therefore, must be kept as sterile as is practical and the burned areas of skin are wrapped in bandages to decrease the risk of infection, stabilize body temperature, minimize loss of body fluids, and permit healing. Therefore, any musical instruments, personnel, sound equipment, or other materials used on the unit in conjunction with music therapy must conform to unit standards and procedures. For example, in view of the danger of using nonsterile headphones or other equipment in critical units, it may be advisable to equip certain rooms with wall mounted speakers or speaker outlets where it is determined that music has been shown to have positive benefits.

Most often there is severe pain associated with burn cases that require hospitalization, as well as with the procedures encountered during treatment. The traditional mode of relief from such pain is to administer morphine or other drugs in dosages that must be, of necessity, insufficient to entirely remove pain sensations. Dosage levels must allow for the fact that the patient must be kept sufficiently alert to cooperate during treatment procedures. However, such pain relievers often carry side effects that present a different set of dangers for the patient. Other aspects of burn therapy that may contribute to the patient's discomfort are daily baths with bandage changes and debridement, as well as the anxiety that accompanies the injury and increases awareness of pain. Every attempt to move and every nursing care procedure is accompanied by pain that increases with improvement in medical condition due to a lowering of the pain threshold (Christenberry, 1979).

MUSIC IN BURN TREATMENT

While music therapy has much to contribute to the emotional, sensory, social, and physical mobility aspects of burn treatment, it is important in relation to Hypothesis 1 to focus on the value of music in decreasing awareness of pain as a constant factor in the reality of a burn patient. Christenberry (1979), a music therapist, has suggested using music to raise pain thresholds and thereby reduce both pain sensations and use of narcotic pain killers with patients on a burn unit of a general hospital. There are four important phases of intervention in which music may be effectively applied:

a. Medical/Physiological Crisis: Music decreases the tension, anxiety, and pain accompanying the early experiencing of serious burn injuries.

b. Treatment/Psychological Emergency: Music decreases the pain associated with debridement, bandage changes or grafting operations, and relieves the isolation and boredom of a sterile environment.

c. Social Emergency: Music structures and enhances communication between the patient, family members, and others during hospitalization and upon discharge.

d. Recovery: Active musical participation helps maintain or restore a positive body image, and stimulates or supports physical therapy activities designed to improve physical function in affected as well as unaffected portions of the body.

Additional research is necessary to objectively establish the full range of musical benefits for burn victims. Such research should address musical effects in all phases of intervention and will be most beneficial when biomedical parameters are the principal focus of data collection.

PAIN CONTROL IN SELECTED GENERAL HOSPITAL UNITS

CANCER TREATMENT

The growing amount of anecdotal and experimental evidence from *oncology* settings suggests that music may have positive benefits in helping cancer patients manage pain. Assuming that the illness has not impaired the function of the periaqueductal gray matter of the thalamus, the nucleus raphe magnus of the medulla, or neurons that send axons to the gray matter of the dorsal horn in the spinal cord, music should be effective as an environmental stimulus in decreasing the ability of the CNS to carry pain stimuli to the brain for conscious awareness. Spintge (1989) has stated that, "Music can be used for anxiolytic and algolytic purposes in the multimodality treatment of cancer pain with great success" (p. 85).

Harvey (1992) related an experience in which music was found to be beneficial for a lady who was dying from cancer of the pancreas and liver, a condition that caused continual pain despite medication. She was also unable to sleep through the night. On an evening near the Christmas season, she participated in about one and one-half hour of singing familiar seasonal songs and subsequently experienced a full night of sleep without pain. The author also reported the results of some research investigations including one in which live music was compared to recorded music as a nonpharmacologic treatment for pain. The live music was found to be superior to tape recorded music in generating significant improvements in physical comfort and tension relief among hospitalized cancer patients. Another study was reported in which listening to music with positive suggestion of pain reduction had an effect on pain perception in patients with chronic cancer pain. However, in such studies care must be taken to isolate the effects as attributable to either music or to verbal suggestion.

Curtis (1986) studied the effect of music on pain relief and relaxation of patients who were diagnosed as having terminal malignant diseases. Although the statistical comparisons did not yield significant effects, analysis of individual responses did indicate possible beneficial effects of music.

Cook (1981) stated her belief that oncology patients could benefit from listening to music via headphones when experiencing pain, nausea, frightening environments, or have lost speaking ability due to surgical removal of the trachea or larynx. She reported the results of a study in which classical music was found effective in reducing the amount of pain medication administered to terminally ill cancer patients at a hospital in Montreal, Canada. Although many studies report that specific types of music are effective, the implication that certain styles of music, or even specific compositions, have predictable differential effects for reducing pain must be tempered with the observation that a wide variety of music has been found effective over several studies. While the human nervous system may respond differentially to separate types of music, it has not been observed to respond identically to a specific composition or style on each listening occasion, nor has its analgesic response to music been isolated to any one style or group of compositions.

A perusal of the literature reveals that in many investigations, music that is selected by, preferred by, or meaningful to the patient has been seen as most effective in bringing about intended results in medical applications (Bailey, 1984; Clark et al., 1981; Cook, 1981; Spintge, 1989). Patients seem to prefer music that has a desirable emotional effect. Such effects are not simply cognitive or purely psychological, they result from feelings generated in human neurophysiological structures. The following chapter is devoted to the biomedical basis of musical influences on emotion and should, therefore, assist in understanding why patients prefer and respond favorably to specific music.

MUSIC IN CORONARY TREATMENT

Placement in the Coronary Care Unit or Intensive Care ward can be an extremely distressing situation for seriously ill patients. Pain, in particular, can be a problem for the cardiac patient when the type of chest pain known as angina pectoris accompanies a heart attack. Spintge (1989) has reported that patients who suffer a cardiac infarction experience marked emotional relaxation and distraction while listening to anxiolytic music. In cardiac rehabilitation, music is used to decrease patient fears of such factors as death or job loss and to motivate the patient to cooperate with the rehabilitation regimen. Music for pain management also appears to be indicated as potentially very beneficial in a coronary care or cardiac rehabilitation unit.

In research by Bonny (1983), both patients and nursing personnel were included in the data gathering process. The purpose was to determine the effectiveness of programmed taped music for reducing stress among nursing personnel on a coronary care unit. Physiological, psychological, and social reactions of patients and staff were measured. Results indicated that heart rate decreases were significant, there was greater tolerance of pain, and patient anxiety and depression were lessened.

MUSIC IN THE PAIN REHABILITATION UNIT

Chronic pain of the type that may not be associated with cardiac illness or cancer is often treated in a Pain Rehabilitation Unit. Wolfe (1978) reported a study done in such a clinic in which pain-related verbalizations were negatively reinforced by ignoring the response, and other verbal responses were socially reinforced by the therapist. Findings showed that patients indulged in prescribed physical activities for increased periods of time, pain-related verbalizations decreased, and positive verbal interaction increased. Although this study does not demonstrate a direct relationship between musical stimuli and pain response, the finding that overt pain responses can be altered through contingent reinforcement may indicate a multiple role for music in pain management as an inhibitor of thalamic pain innervation, as a reinforcer for related behaviors, and as a means of structuring physical and social activity for patients of chronic pain.

NEXT

Nearly all of the authors and investigators who have studied pain management and pain-related behavior acknowledge the major role played by the patient's emotional state in the degree of pain perceived. In the following chapter, the biomedical basis for the use of music in this important area of patient behavior is examined.

V

MUSICAL EFFECTS
ON CRANIAL CENTERS
FOR EMOTION

A mong the hospital patients and psychiatric clients who are seen in music therapy practice, nearly all exhibit evidence of an emotional component in addition to the physical injury or illness, cognitive disability, perceptual disorder, or motor impairment that constitutes the primary clinical pathology. Research and clinical reports of patients undergoing treatment in surgery, emergency, burn center, obstetrics, dialysis, pediatrics, trauma center, intensive care, oncology, cardiac rehabilitation, and hospice as well as clients in psychiatry, centers for the developmentally disabled, extended care facilities, and educational institutions include data reflecting the superior efficacy of treatment when the subject's emotional state is under control. These reports often describe the successful use of music as a catalyst in fostering a cooperative, positive, and predictable emotional state.

Although published accounts include information on the people whose emotional responses are affected, the types of music used to bring about desired results, and the framework within which the music is utilized, none as yet has described exactly *how* music generates such changes in human emotional behavior. An understanding of musical influences on intracranial processing of emotional responses is needed before informed decisions can be made that will lead to more accurate and predictable applications of music to affect emotional responses.

Neurological processing of musical sound was discussed in Chapter 3 and included a discussion of the structures through which sound energy passes on its way to the auditory cortex. That information, along with data to be provided in this section, lead to the theoretical premise reflected in Hypothesis 2 of the Biomedical Theory of Music Therapy:

> The normal neurological pathway for sound sensation allows music to have an effect on those structures in the human brain most responsible for emotional behavior, the hypothalamus and limbic system, thereby inhibiting negative emotional reactions which can delay or otherwise interfere with the treatment or recovery process.

There are three aspects of emotion that professionals must confront in dealing with patients in a clinical setting. These are the feeling component, emotional expression, and responses to the expressions of others. When individuals exhibit emotional behaviors that indicate strong emotional upheaval, efforts are made to help calm them during periods of crisis. If the behaviors are inappropriate or unacceptable to members of the surrounding society, the individuals have been labeled as emotionally disturbed or as having a behavior disorder. In the latter case, the assumption is that the observed emotional expression or response is due to a distorted feeling response, lack of feelings, inability to recognize or properly identify emotional feelings, or unwillingness to reveal one's true emotional state to others. When music is used to help correct problematic emotional behavior, its primary effects are neurological and biochemical, with secondary effects resulting in subjective awarenesses, changes in emotional cognition, and behavioral responses. The following section examines these effects.

NEUROPSYCHOLOGY OF EMOTION AND MUSIC

THE COMPONENTS OF EMOTION

Any single emotional response consists of three components: behavioral, autonomic, and hormonal (Carlson, 1992). When muscles move in response to a situation, behavior becomes observable and provides information regarding the behavioral component of an individual's emotional makeup. Autonomic (ANS) responses provide rapid mobilization of energy to facilitate the behaviors. During an episode of emotional excitement, the sympathetic branch of the ANS increases its activity while the parasympathetic branch decreases. As a result, heart rate increases and blood vessels dilate or constrict to circulate blood toward skeletal muscles and away from the digestive system. Hormonal secretions of epinephrine and norepinephrine reinforce autonomic responses by further increasing blood flow to the muscles and causing glycogen stored in the muscles to be converted to glucose. A similar effect may be generated using music to increase muscle tone as described in Chapter 3. When a therapist can successfully initiate such a response using music, the feelings and behavioral responses of an individual may be examined to facilitate awareness and explore needed alternative response possibilities.

Although musically stimulated neural changes appear to affect a wide range of neurological structures, the overt behaviors, autonomic responses, and hormonal secretions that comprise emotion are controlled by separate neurological systems. The amygdala appears to be the integrating mechanism for controlling these responses (Carlson, 1992). The amygdala is a limbic structure located in the temporal lobe and is responsible for behavioral reactions to objects or stimuli that are perceived to be of special biological significance. It serves as the focal point between sensory systems, such as the auditory reception system for music, and effector systems that are responsible for the three components of emotion. The amygdala, therefore, also governs reactions to perceived situations involving anticipated pain or fear of bodily harm. Its role is to organize emotional responses generated by perceived or anticipated aversive stimuli. It is particularly well situated to do this because it receives its information through neuronal projections from the inferior temporal lobe and the temporal pole at the end of the temporal lobe. These two regions receive information from visual, auditory, and somatosensory association areas of the brain, thereby keeping the amygdala well informed about what is occurring in the surrounding environment.

MUSICALLY CONDITIONED EMOTIONAL RESPONSES

An often used treatment for the negative emotional responses that accompany aversive stimuli is to provide an alternative stimulus and condition the subject to experience an alternative emotional reaction. This procedure is effective because emotional responses, like many other types of responses, can be conditioned by experience (Carlson, 1992). For example, when an individual learns through experience that childbirth or oral surgery may be painful, that person may exhibit fear, escape-avoidance behavior, or the immobilizing "freeze" response upon encountering that situation. Also occurring will be autonomic responses that normally attend such emotional responses, such as blood pressure, pupillary dilation, heart and respiratory rate changes, and release of stress-related hormones. Development of this type of conditioned emotional response requires activity in the central nucleus of the amygdala. The lateral hypothalamus is also involved with blood pressure changes and release of stress hormones, and the periaqueductal gray matter of the thalamus with the freeze response. If, however, the individual experiences properly applied musical intervention concurrent with the fearful situation, these same structures will be involved in processing musical stimuli and the person will become conditioned to associate the experience with auditory aesthetics, positive associations, and decreased pain awareness, and the autonomic changes, avoidance behaviors, and hormonal secretions will not occur.

The thalamus is particularly important in any consideration of conditioned emotional responses because the medial geniculate nucleus is located there. Not only does the medial geniculate nucleus serve as the final relay station for sending auditory information to the brain, its medial division is also required for learning conditioned emotional responses involving auditory cues (Carlson, 1992). This makes music even more integral to the process of conditioning emotional behaviors that will be supportive of treatment procedures, in addition to its functions of raising the pain threshold and arousing the brain to focus attention away from seemingly harmful stimuli.

The orbitofrontal cortex, located at the base of the frontal lobes, is another structure that plays a role in emotional responses. It receives input from the thalamus, temporal cortex, amygdala, the olfactory system, and other parts of the frontal lobes. It affects a wide variety of emotional and other physiological responses through its projections to the cingulate gyrus of the cortex, hippocampal system, temporal cortex, lateral hypothalamus, and amygdala. Among the emotional responses that are attributed to the orbitofrontal cortex are some that have been found in practice to be responsive to intervention through music. They include personal inhibitions and self-concerns, worries about the consequences of one's actions, overt emotional reactions to pain, and creating appropriate feelings and behaviors based on other brain centers' judgments and conclusions about events. The efforts of the therapist in these areas of function are aimed, therefore, at reconditioning the emotional responses that are governed by the orbitofrontal cortex. An example of such an application of musical influences was contained in a *Billboard* commentary report by Craig Chaquico (1995), former guitarist with Jefferson Starship. He reported on a 17-year-old girl with cancer who was wheelchair-bound and whose concerns and inhibitions had made her so depressed and withdrawn that she did not talk to staff or family members. Then a music therapist brought in an omnichord, an electronic musical instrument designed to allow even non-musicians to make music. When the patient was given an omnichord lesson, her mother reported that she exhibited happiness for the first time since entering the hospital. While not a cure for the cancer, music therapy did help her cope emotionally with the disease and its associated clinical isolation.

The hippocampal formation, in particular, receives information from the amygdala and exchanges information through the intorhinal cortex with all association areas of the brain, as well as with subcortical regions that include axons which produce noradrenalin, serotonin, and acetylcholine. Respectively, these neurotransmitters mediate alertness, control of eating, and excitation of skeletal muscle, all of which are involved in the behaviors that formulate goals and objectives related to emotion in music therapy practice.

Although not considered a part of the limbic system, the cingulate gyrus is surrounded by limbic structures and stimulation of this region results in both positive and negative emotions in humans. It appears to mediate the decision making functions of the frontal lobes, emotional functions of the limbic system, and control of movement by the motor cortex. Its role is to excite the centers for emotion and stimulate motivation (Carlson, 1992). Therefore, in therapeutic applications, planned decision making during musical participation, musically motivated emotional reactions, and musically stimulated motor activity can be facilitated in part by stimulation of the cingulate gyrus via holologic auditory processing as described in Chapter 3.

Accurate recognition of emotional expressions by others involves seeing, hearing and interpreting facial expressions, voice quality, word choice, and body language. Carlson (1992) has described several studies showing that the right hemisphere appears to be dominant in comprehension of emotional expression, and some indicating that the right hemisphere also is more expressive than the left. However, the right side of the cortex does not control physical expressions of emotion. Facial expressions, including laughing and crying, are initiated by neural circuits in the brain stem. These circuits are controlled by the frontal lobes which guide and place limits on the amount of emotional expression to be displayed.

In interpreting the expressions of others, habitual misidentification of the emotions of peers or family members has strong potential for serious problems in interpersonal relationships (Carlson, 1992). Music therapists encountering clients whose emotional reactions appear inappropriate to the expressions of others must address the brain's capabilities for emotional cognition.

Because of the capability for musical stimulation of emotional centers in the brain, there is good potential for generating new conditioned emotional responses in the client's behavioral repertoire.

BRAIN REINFORCEMENT AND MUSICAL STIMULI

In those cases in which the desire is to calm one's emotional state, efforts are made through music or ideational stimuli to generate positive (rather than negative) emotions. Positive emotions tend to be associated with stimuli that serve as reinforcers of behavior. People generally tend to feel positively toward objects or people that serve as environmental sources of reinforcement. Consequently, they seek out and often form a degree of dependence on such reinforcers. If that resource becomes unable to continue as a source of reinforcement, or if the immediate situation is perceived as unrewarding or harmful, a readily available, nonthreatening, noninvasive environmental source of immediate reinforcement is needed in order to elicit a positive attitude that will strengthen, rather than weaken, chances for success in the treatment and recovery process. Music has been found to be an effective environmental stimulus in generating positive emotional feelings and expressions in human beings. Data to be presented later in this chapter will demonstrate the beneficial effects of utilizing the reinforcing effects of music in both physical medicine and psychiatric interventions.

How does music arouse such feelings independently in the behavior of individuals who may find themselves in quite unreinforcing circumstances? The answer to this question lies in the way the brain is stimulated to produce behaviors in response to other reinforcing objects. Investigators believe that the reinforcement system is activated by the awareness and acquisition of natural reinforcers such as food, water, or sexual contact. The system activates behavior which connects the perception of a reinforcer with the performance of a reinforcing act, such as actually eating the food upon perceiving that it is available. In this way, reinforcers act to elicit behavior (Carlson, 1992).

Music activates the same neuropsychological system. However, there is no need to use awareness of the object to motivate the person to perform a reinforcing act because the awareness is integral with the reinforcing effects. When a person becomes aware of music through audition, the music is already stimulating the production of reinforcing impulses and biochemical substances within the brain. Its reinforcement value is readily observed in its ability to elicit the same "appetitive" responses that are consistently exhibited in response to other objects that produce reinforcing brain stimulation. These behaviors are specifically aimed at acquiring the objects that are found to be reinforcing. A person who hears music and who experiences feelings of reinforcement will not only allow such music to continue while responding with positive expressions of emotion, but also will actively seek the same or similar musical stimuli when confronted with an opportunity to do so.

Findings regarding the biochemical aspects of reinforcement serve to further illuminate the basis of the reinforcing effects of music. The brain produces neural impulses, neurotransmitters, and endogenous morphines (also called endogenous opioids or endorphins) that generate feelings of reinforcement. Endogenous opioids stimulate opiate receptors which activate neurons involved in creating feelings of reinforcement. In particular, dopamine is active in the reinforcement process. The mechanism appears to involve norepinephrine and dopamine receptors in responding to the effects of appetitive stimuli (food, drink, mating partner). The reinforcement is initiated by feedback from indulgence in appetitive behavior such as eating, drinking, or mating, thereby strengthening the link between the stimulus and the response.

The neural pathway that appears to play the most important role in reinforcement contains neurons whose terminal buttons secrete dopamine and which culminates in the nucleus accumbens, a region in the basal forebrain whose nerve cells act as dopamine receptors. Stimulation of this area is very reinforcing and is responsible for the reinforcing effects of appetitive stimuli. Carlson has stated that "any treatment that stimulates dopamine receptors in the nucleus accumbens will reinforce behaviors" (p. 504). It is generally accepted among investigators that reinforcement results from activating dopamine receptors in the nucleus accumbens. Because music, through the brain's hololigic processing mechanisms, can simultaneously reach large segments of the brain with sustained stimulation, it appears to be capable of stimulating both dopaminergic (dopamine producing) neurons and dopamine receptor areas with impulses that are sufficiently reinforcing to cause music to have reinforcing value that is useful, observable, and replicable. Application of this principle allows music to induce feelings and expressions of positive emotions independent of other reinforcing stimuli.

EMOTIONAL COGNITION AND MUSICAL INFLUENCES

In discussing the neuropsychological processes involved in musical perception, Roederer (1985) points out that motivational and emotional responses are controlled in structures of the limbic system working together with cortical networks of cognition. The limbic system is activated by environmental stimuli, by images formulated through thinking, and by somatic input. The system uses motivation and emotion to assure that all cortical processes are carried out so as to bring maximum benefit to the organism. It does so by dispensing impulses and substances that produce sensations of reward or punishment whenever the organism observes that its own behavioral acts have enhanced or diminished chances of survival of the organism and the species.

Because cortical structures that conduct cognitive operations are involved in perception and expression of emotional responses, a term, "emotional cognition" is needed to acknowledge and refer to this relationship. Various theories have appeared to explain how music generates emotional responses. Some are based upon the assumption that cognitive aspects of musical perception can be used to explain and perhaps predict human emotional responses. One such theory (Bever, 1988) places the emphasis on cultural experience as the source of most expectations generated while listening to music. As one gains increasingly more experience with the music of a culture, the brain stores information concerning progressions of sounds used commonly in that society. As a result, the brain begins to form expectations about upcoming musical sounds based on information collected previously. When a sequence of musical tones or harmonies is apprehended, the brain is aroused by the expectation of certain sounds that, in all probability, should follow the tones already heard. Some of these expectations are fulfilled and some are not fulfilled. The amount of emotional pleasure is dependent upon the arousal level generated by the tension between expectation and fulfillment of expected musical events.

Meyer (1967) acknowledged that the tension created by conflict between expected and observed musical progressions provides substantial opportunity for experiencing and expressing emotions. He attempted, however, to use information theory to create a quasi-quantifiable theory of emotional probability. His theory focused on the ability of the brain to expect certain sounds based on the repetition frequency of those sounds. According to his ideas, sounds that are often repeated tend to be expected more, and they produce relaxation when heard. If there are too many sounds used to create a musical message, there may be too many separate bits of information to present, thus allowing too little repetition of any specific ones for the brain to determine which ones to expect in any given sequence. Consequently, the relationship between tension and relaxation will be much more difficult to establish and utilize as a basis for musical expectations. Unexpected musical events tend to create or sustain tension, thereby stimulating various emotions. According to this model, when a musical event occurs, the degree to which that musical event is unexpected will determine the amount of arousal that contributes to an emotional response.

Research and clinical studies reported in the following section describe beneficial uses of the emotional power of music in general hospital applications. They reflect the biomedical principles related previously in this chapter and are representative of the use of music to stimulate emotional centers in the brain as indicated in Hypothesis 2.

CONTROLLING EMOTIONS WITH MUSIC
IN PHYSICAL MEDICINE

Not only does the trauma of physical injury carry with it substantial emotional trauma, but the treatment and recovery processes can also be emotionally destabilizing. As Wilson (1988) has indicated, serious illness or injury always leave emotional scars in their wake. Some emotional damage may result from feelings of failure to keep one's physical apparatus free from harm. Recovery of physical control requires a great deal of self motivation to discover and master physical, emotional and intellectual integrity. Too often, the patient is counseled to accept his or her condition when the physician has nothing more to offer. Wilson contends that the music therapist, however, offers the message "that a handicap ceases to exist as a physical reality when it has been vanquished as a psychological reality" (p. 140). This is the powerful emotional appeal of musical participation for the patient suffering from a physical disease.

ORGAN TRANSPLANTS

While modern medical science has advanced to the point that transplanting body parts between individuals no longer occupies major time and space in the media, the emotional components of an organ transplant experience have not received corresponding attention from the scientific community. Gibbons and McDougal (1983) reviewed a number of reports that illuminated the emotional components in organ transplant operations for the donor, recipient, and family. They reported that both emotional and social adjustment factors are associated with prognosis, pain, medical procedures, and quality of life as measured in physical parameters during posttransplant recovery periods. Because many preferred donors are family members, there often are high stress levels, guilt feelings, and family conflicts with which to contend. Resulting disturbances may include regressive behavior, uncontrolled anger, depression, anxiety, and refusal to cooperate. Emotional problems related to treatment can result from days of isolation in a sterile environment with sensory deprivation, long periods of unstructured time, and without interpersonal closeness, all of which can lead to emotional problems so severe that they interfere with the surgical process. During the posttransplant stage, there may be fears of transplant rejection by one's own immune system, and anxiety about the possibility of death or possible additional procedures such as dialysis or another transplant.

Gibbons and McDougal suggest that music therapy may be an effective way to confront transplant-related stressors using music as a transitional mode of communication, as a noninvasive catalyst to elicit physical sedation, and as an environmental source of reinforcement. As an example, they report a study in which music was used to significantly reduce hypertension and some medication dosages. They also suggest that music be used to structure stable and predictable situations for families to reduce stress and distract attention from the trauma as well as to improve self-concept and stimulate arousal in the transplant recipient.

ONCOLOGY

Bailey (1984) has reported the feelings of isolation, depression, tension, loss, grief, and pain experienced by patients in a cancer setting. Into this atmosphere of negative emotions and anticipation of further pain, the music therapist enters with objectives focused upon release of tension and recovery of feelings of control, comfort and relaxation. The therapist's real task is to recondition the brain, in particular the amygdala, to facilitate more positive coping responses in the presence or anticipated presence of aversive aspects of cancer and its treatment. In addition, the music therapist wishes to stimulate the hypothalamus to engage in activities other than allowing increased secretions of stress hormones, and the cingulate gyrus to elicit behaviors other than those that indicate continuous pain awareness.

To accomplish these objectives musical activities are used which, by design, necessitate togetherness among family members and which carry positive associations with people, places, and events in the patient's life. Such experiences and songs can be quite reinforcing in the sense described in an earlier section of this chapter, and they carry with them the same potential for arousal and motivation. Through the planned use of musical interventions the patient may acquire the interpersonal closeness and aesthetic stimulation that are so often lacking in the sterile, technological environments associated with modern medical treatment. Songs having personalized connections with positive reminiscences, needs and desires, interpersonal relationships, and even loss and death are described by Bailey as effective in helping patient and family members resolve issues and diminish feelings of isolation and fear.

In the abstract of her presentation to the Seventh World Congress of Music Therapy in 1993, Anne Olofsson described the effects of musical applications in the oncological clinic at the Karolinska Hospital in Stockholm, Sweden. She reported that music alone was used to prevent and alleviate side effects of chemotherapy and, in combination with other forms of intervention, contributed to relief of insomnia or states of tension, encouragement of physical awareness and acceptance, and creation of contacts between patients and with relatives. The biomedical basis of such positive interactions is readily discernible in the motivation to secure repeated and continued access to the source of stimulation that produces sensations of reinforcement while engaged in music as a common endeavor with others. Both the relaxing effects and the physical awareness result from the ability of music to directly access neuronal activity in the autonomic nervous system through arousal mechanisms mediated in the midbrain and brain stem.

PEDIATRICS

Among the areas of physical medicine that have received attention in music therapy literature, the pediatrics unit has been the focus of much study. The emotional components of unexpected hospitalization can be quite profound in children. Rudenberg and Royka (1989) reported on the effects of music therapy in conjunction with child life therapy for pediatric burn patients. Issues faced by the children and their families resulted in various emotional states experienced during hospitalization and were met through therapeutic goals designed to help them cope with multiple losses, work through invasive and painful medical procedures, reinforce physical/occupational goals, increase lung capacity, and adapt to successive stages of recovery. The losses can be quite traumatic and may include loss of normal body self-concept, lives of other loved ones, mobility, peer group, and school-related experiences. Such losses often represent important sources of reinforcement in the child's life.

Feelings of reinforcement can be regained from an environmental source by using music to help the children experience success and positive reminiscences while simultaneously expressing their feelings through songwriting as a transitional object. Through its effects on the autonomic nervous system music assists in both emotional and physical relaxation as the child is subjected to surgery, tubbings, dressing changes, and exercises during treatment. Musical games can be created to familiarize the child with a procedure prior to the actual experience. Increases in lung capacity after inhalation injury may be gained through exercises involving music to accompany blowing a balloon, move an object a given distance, or to play a wind instrument such as a pianica.

Children who are resistive to movement in physical therapy due to the intense pain associated with such efforts may be motivated to move more readily with adapted musical instruments or songs involving actions. Use of such instruments may include strumming an autoharp or playing a pianica or other keyboard instrument with one's toes (Rudenberg & Royka, 1989). The positive emotions experienced through musically elicited relaxation, familiarization, success, and motivation have proven to be quite valuable during the treatment process. Benefits include helping the child and family cope with losses, working through painful and invasive treatment procedures, supporting occupational and physical therapy goals, increasing lung capacity, and facilitating psychological adaptation during various stages of recovery. Additional biomedical examination of the values of music for treating anxiety in pediatric patients is included in Chapter 8.

Injuries requiring hospital admission are severe and quite unexpected. Therefore the experience may be particularly overwhelming to a child. The child's psychological adjustment to the hospital may be affected by relationships with parents, factors that contributed to the injury, and feelings of guilt among the child and family. McDonnell (1984) has reported on the use of music therapy with two victims of physical assault, one of whom sustained a fracture and one who was burned. Deprived of basic comforting interactions such as physical closeness, musical experiences provide valuable compensation by providing the child with a sense of safety and security upon seeing the parents in a less worried mode while sharing musical sounds, rhythm, and positive associations suggested by familiar songs. This objective as well as increased and more effective communication between parents and child were achieved through musical games involving props manipulated by parents and child, and original lyrics relating to the immediate situation as well as to other circumstances in the lives of the family.

Pediatric Case Studies

Through case study reports, Perez (1989) has related her use of music as a Child Life Specialist in addressing sadness, anger, and joy in children and adolescents admitted to Children's Memorial Medical Center in Chicago for treatment of physical illness or disability. Traumatic awarenesses associated with illness, hospitalization and treatment were interfering with their abilities to think, feel, act and proceed with psychosocial development. The music therapist's objectives included building a trusting relationship, providing opportunities for enjoyment, learning about the self and the new environment, and dealing with overwhelming emotions. While the author personifies music by stating that it conveys emotion, a biomedical explanation does not assume that music has emotions to convey. Rather, it is recognized that patterns of neural innervation associated with musical experience stimulate certain cranial structures and processes. This stimulation results in changes in mood, affective behavior, and feeling experiences.

In one case, an 18-year-old female being treated for leukemia was described as exhibiting increasing sadness associated with repeated failure of her medications to send her illness back into remission. Her smiles and other forms of positive emotional expressiveness were restored while listening to a string quartet by Ravel and holding hands with the therapist. In another case, a six-year-old boy harbored a great deal of anger at himself after a fall from a three story building, and he began to project this anger onto others in the environment. He was able to identify the source and object of his anger through original song lyrics created with the help of the music therapist. He was then able to express more genuine positive emotions and to decrease his previously hostile behavior. In the case of an 11-year-old girl, a hormonal imbalance had precipitated a psychotic episode. The music therapist used music and creative movement to reestablish normal verbal and nonverbal communication with the patient.

In the Discussion section of her paper, Perez asks a very important question: "Is there a unifying theory on which the clinical use of music is based?" (p. 246). Her answer is a very certain "no" and she argues against any efforts to create one model of understanding. Instead she encourages openness to all views claiming as her own theoretical base a many faceted ideology that mentions the ideas of Carl Rogers as a humanist, philosophies of Heraclitus and Lao Tzu linked to modern physics, biology, and the social sciences, Process Theory of Monism with its triune composition of energy, matter, and information, Jacob Moreno's psychodrama theories, and psychoanalytic techniques, although she rejects both the cathartic clinical premises of psychoanalysis and the application of behavioral theories to music therapy.

While the case studies reported by Perez may appear to represent no collective premise that would explain the basis for the effects observed, it may be that the premise simply had not been identified at the time the paper was written. When a sound premise can be identified, case studies such as those described above will no longer be seen as individual examples of unexplained, unpredictable chance occurrences that happened to hit upon an incomprehensible something that helped in these isolated instances. The value of a unifying theoretical basis for the observed clinical effects of music is that it provides every therapist with the ability to explain musical benefits as predictable and replicable gains that can be experienced by a significant majority of similarly afflicted patients. The logical explanation of these cases resides in the biomedical description (provided in early sections of this chapter) of the effects of musical stimulation on the hypothalamus, forebrain sections of the frontal lobes, limbic structures and areas that connect with structures whose specific functions are to generate emotional responses both on the feeling and expressive levels of behavior.

HEMODIALYSIS

An important objective with many procedures in physical medicine is to have emotions under sufficient control that blood pressure will not be a problem during invasive procedures. Invasive treatment requires that the medical staff invade the body by breaking its outer covering to directly access internal organs. One such procedure that numerous patients must undergo repeatedly is a blood cleansing procedure known as "hemodialysis." When kidney disease causes the kidneys to be no longer able to accomplish this task and a kidney transplant cannot be performed, the alternatives are continuous ambulatory peritoneal dialysis (CAPD) or an artificial kidney machine. During hemodialysis, the patient's blood passes through a semipermeable membranous tube which is surrounded by a balanced salt solution. Waste products are extracted from the blood or needed substances can be added to the blood. Patients using the artificial kidney machine experience multi-hour procedures about two times per week (Mader, 1995).

The problem in hemodialysis is the frequent fluctuation between hypertension and hypotension during treatment. During stress, blood pressure may be influenced by actions of the endocrine and nervous systems. Schuster (1985) reported a study in which patient-selected tape recorded music was introduced thirty minutes following the onset of treatment and continued for 1 hour. This was followed by 1 hour of no music and subsequently 1 hour of music listening by patients in the experimental group. Blood pressure measurements were taken after each hour of treatment. Although both the experimental and control group readings declined gradually as dialysis progressed, the statistical analysis revealed that experimental group systolic pressure was significantly lower at the onset of dialysis and diastolic pressure was significantly lower than control group pressure during the second reading. It was suggested that awareness of the opportunity to listen to music may have precipitated reduced anxiety in experimental group subjects.

Biomedical data supports Schuster's interpretation with further explanation of the specific structures and pathways through which the musical influences accomplished their effects. Specifically, the music therapist utilizes interventions that involve the amygdala and hypothalamus with reactions to musical stimuli instead of with the blood pressure changes and release of stress-related hormones that would accompany perception of an aversive stimulus in the absence of music. With musically stimulated impulses occupying neural pathways throughout the brain, the orbitofrontal cortex is less able to focus on self-concerns in determining emotional responses. The positive responses are sustained and replicated as the individual's brain stores conditioned emotional responses resulting from the effects of music on the medial division of the medial geniculate nucleus in the thalamus (See "Musically Conditioned Emotional Responses" above).

This chapter has focused primarily on biomedical accounts of music therapy applications in medical-surgical settings. The remaining sections will present biomedical foundations of music as a therapeutic modality with psychiatric clients.

BIOMEDICAL DETERMINANTS
OF CONTROL REVERSAL THERAPY

Professional literature describing therapeutic uses of music contains examples and explanations of clinical progress with persons referred for treatment of such maladies as borderline personality disorder, bipolar disorder, obsessive compulsive disorder, severe depression, and schizophrenia. However, a very serious class of diseases, eating disorders, has received comparatively little attention from those seeking to provide a literary basis for music therapy practices, although much work has been done clinically (Parente, 1989). In recent years, a music therapy based technique known as "Control Reversal Therapy" has been designed, described, and utilized with very positive results with patients. To understand the basis of this new technique, it is necessary to examine first the psychological and biological components of eating disorders as they have been described, and to extend these interpretations to those factors that are addressed through application of biomedical influences of music on the brains of eating disorders patients.

EATING DISORDERS: ANOREXIA AND BULIMIA

Eating disorders have been seen with disturbing frequency in music therapy clinics throughout the country and beyond. The most common eating disorders are bulimia and anorexia nervosa, the latter of which is found to be fatal for one patient in thirty. Anorexia primarily affects young adolescent females and is characterized by refusal to eat. However, anorexics are usually preoccupied with food and enjoy preparing meals for others to eat, collecting recipes, and hoarding food that they do not eat. They express an intense fear of becoming obese and indulge in exercises such as cycling, running, constant walking and pacing. Many suffer from osteoporosis and their bones are more susceptible than normal to fractures. If weight loss becomes severe, the menstrual cycle ceases.

When controls on food intake fail, they may gorge themselves with food, a behavior known as bulimia. This type of binge is followed by self-induced vomiting, use of laxatives, and feelings of depression and guilt. When repeated episodes of bulimia occur without anorexia, the condition is known as bulimia nervosa. A drug called fenfluramine has often been successful in treating bulimia nervosa, but experts have so far learned of no reliable treatment for anorexia (Carlson, 1992).

The search for causes of anorexia nervosa has prompted many observers to adopt the belief that because the disease primarily affects young women, it is due to an overreaction to society's emphasis on slimness as a standard of beauty in young women. However, other factors reported in studies of anorexics show that the physiological and psychological correlates of the disease are much more involved. Carlson (1992) has reported studies indicating that CT scans of anorexics reveal enlarged ventricles and widened sulci, both of which are indicative of loss of brain tissue. The widened sulci appear to return to normal upon recovery, but not the enlarged ventricles. Other studies show evidence of changes in two monoamines that affect behavior, norepinephrine and serotonin, the latter of which is involved in control of eating. It is believed, however, that these changes may be effects rather than causes of the disease.

The personality characteristics accompanying anorexia are usually found in women. They include perfectionism, excessive worry, need for control, inflexibility, panic attacks, and internal dialogue (Parente, 1989). In interviews or through therapy, a very common factor revealed in the backgrounds of these patients is a major loss such as the unexpected loss of an environmental source of reinforcement, or feelings of loss of control of one's personal autonomy and social integrity following an episode such as physical or sexual abuse. Experiences of this type usually are followed by serious emotional instability involving feelings of loss of control and low self-esteem with depressive reactions. One of the many forms of therapy used in treating this disease focuses upon helping the anorexic patient identify and change the faulty belief systems that she applies to herself and to her environment. Once new beliefs are adopted, the therapist assists the patient in learning to use the new emotional self-help skills in situations outside of the therapy setting. A difficulty with this approach is the excessive amount of denial practiced by these highly intelligent patients, often taking the form of a very convincing pretense of adopting the new thought patterns.

THE BIOLOGY OF ANOREXIA

There is a long-held view that the hypothalamus is involved in the control of food intake, and that peptide hormones help regulate eating and drinking. Anorexia would be simple to treat if therapy could directly utilize the repeated finding that eating behavior is increased by stimulation of the lateral hypothalamus (Thompson, 1967), particularly when stimulation occurs through infusion of a neurotransmitter called "neuropeptide Y" into the mid-lateral hypothalamus resulting in frantic, ravenous eating (Carlson, 1992). Levels of neuropeptide Y in the hypothalamus do tend to increase during food deprivation, but its effect is not sufficient to motivate the anorexic patient to resume eating.

While many investigators continue to focus on the biological and social control of feeding and metabolism as the sources of a potential cure for anorexia, others have concluded that "eating is not the fundamental problem of people with anorexia. Rather, being out of control in all areas of their lives—physiological, emotional, mental, and behavioral—is the primary feature of anorexia" (Parente, p. 44, 1989). The compound effect of this continuous perceived lack of control coupled with the absence of incoming nutrients results in an attack of incomprehensible proportions on the body's ability to sustain itself.

The more an individual feels that the situation cannot be controlled, the stronger will be the stress reaction experienced by that individual. Stress in this context refers to the physiological reaction caused by the continuous perception of threatening situations. The perception that the external forces governing one's life cannot be controlled generates a sustained stress reaction consisting of autonomic and endocrine responses designed to mobilize the body's energy resources. Consequently, the adrenal glands secrete epinephrine which affects glucose metabolism, norepinephrine which is a hormone that increases heart output and blood pressure, and steroid stress hormones such as cortisol. Cortisol is a glucocorticoid that also profoundly affects glucose metabolism, helps break down protein and convert it to glucose, increases blood flow, and stimulates behavioral responses through its presumed effects on the brain. Sustained stress, such as that experienced by anorexics who feel out of control of their lives, results in prolonged secretion of glucocorticoids with damaging long-term effects. High blood pressure, increased risk of heart attacks and strokes, steroid diabetes, infertility, inhibition of the inflammatory response, and suppression of the immune system are some of the known effects of elevated blood levels of glucocorticoids. (See Chapter 8 for detailed explanation of glucocorticoid effects on the immune system.) Research has shown that prolonged exposure to glucocorticoids destroys neurons in one zone of the hippocampus by making them susceptible to potentially harmful events such as decreased blood flow, and by lowering their ability to utilize glucose. As blood flow decreases, these cells cannot sustain sufficient metabolic activity to remain alive (Carlson, 1992).

Anorexic behavior intensifies the problem by omitting dietary sources of protein that the glucocorticoid cortisol would help break down and convert to glucose for use by brain cells. During times when protein cannot be absorbed from the digestive tract, the brain lives on glucose drawn from the body's carbohydrate reservoir. When carbohydrate reservoirs in the liver are depleted, the brain and the rest of the body must live on fatty acids drawn from the fat reservoir as long as the individual allows some fat to remain in the body, a concession that is simply unacceptable to the anorexic patient.

DEVELOPMENT OF "CONTROL REVERSAL THERAPY" FOR ANOREXIA

As described above, the probability and severity of a stress reaction is very much dependent upon perception of the degree to which a situation can be controlled. Part of the behavioral response to a perceived lack of control is often to substitute control of one aspect of a person's life for the absence of control over events in other aspects of life in general. In interviews and in therapy sessions with anorexic patients by this author, the problem of control is nearly always expressed along with statements revealing extreme frustration in efforts to successfully regain control from external forces exerting their will on the patient's life. The constant control of eating behavior seems, therefore, to have been adopted as a source of internal control, a transference device that provides an illusion of more pervasive control in the life of the anorexic patient. It does not, however, remove the awareness of external controls or the resulting stress reaction.

Because the issue of being out of control appeared as a recurrent theme in assessment and treatment of anorexia, it was decided that a form of treatment that reversed the locus of control and put it in the hands of the patient may offer an effective procedure for confronting the disease. This provided the impetus for the music therapy procedure called "Control Reversal Therapy" (CRT), which has been used with great success in clinical applications since 1988. All referrals have been made by the patients themselves, all patients have been female, and all have received individual treatment.

CRT Procedure

The process begins with an assessment interview during which the patient is allowed to volunteer any information on the history of her illness, its manifestations in her physical functioning or overt behavior, any correlates with the illness such as changes in relationships with significant others, obsessive thoughts of food or of controlling food intake, prior interventions, and musical abilities or interests. This information is used by the author as therapist to verify that a significant amount of the typical symptomatology is present to indicate anorexia nervosa as the primary pathology. However, only the issue of control and data on the patient's musical background were used in setting session objectives or planning musical interventions. Typical issues such as body image, perfectionism, food intake volume, body weight, and personal insight are considered secondary to the primary goal of regaining internal control over situations in the patient's life.

The interview is followed by a session in which the patient is placed in control of a musical activity and is allowed to participate on her own terms. This experience often takes place during the initial meeting to both assess her musical behavior, her current ability or lack of ability to be in control of a situation, and early on to fulfill her expectations for *music* as part of the treatment in this setting. While this initial experience was not originally intended to have verifiable treatment effects, patients have exhibited and reported substantial changes in emotions and self image following just one CRT experience during their first visit. Such early positive gains were both unexpected and explainable using musical influence data available at the time the procedure began to be used in 1988.

Treatment typically proceeds in subsequent sessions with extremely positive and very rapidly achieved results. The objective is to always transfer the patient's perceived locus of control from forces in her environment over to herself as the primary agent of control. Patients often arrive at sessions complaining of feeling depressed, sometimes accompanied by suicidal ideation. Each session is designed to use actual experiences to generate feelings of internal control. Materials for musical activity are made available by the therapist, and are planned according to the needs of each patient to address sources of control in her life. Each experience begins whenever the patient feels comfortable with the opportunity and decides to start. It continues in whatever musical direction she decides to go and is allowed to continue until she independently decides to stop, generally between 20 and 45 minutes after beginning.

There are many readily available sources of continuous control in music therapy. Some of these techniques include a) the patient teaches the therapist how to play or sing certain songs, b) the patient teaches the therapist how to play an instrument, c) the patient uses a rhythm instrument to signal and control the therapist's improvisatory playing of various instruments, d) the patient writes the words to a song about a relevant topic, and she and the therapist set the lyrics to music with each note subject to selection and approval by the patient, e) the patient creates music using interactive computer programs that provide control of on-screen, musical, and printed output, or f) the patient is allowed to select and place instruments around the therapy area representing important people in her life. In the latter activity, patients have been asked to improvise, first to show how each of those individuals normally interacts in the patient's life, and then to play each instrument as she would like to have each individual express himself/herself if she, the patient, were to be able to control that person's interactions. This can be a very powerful therapeutic technique and should not be used as a format early in the sequence of sessions.

Observed CRT Outcomes

In an initial CRT experience, the session typically has three rather clearly identifiable segments: In phase one the patient is put in control of the therapist and she reluctantly gives directions and signals changes while giving the clear impression that she has no expectation that her directives will be carried out. In phase two she realizes that she really *is* in control and exhibits new confidence in giving directives and signals. The third phase begins when she starts to relinquish control back to the therapist, appears to decide that she likes and wishes to stay in the role that she has assumed, and usually moves in a very obvious and assertive way to sustain her position of control for a longer time. Occasionally, the latter segment can be the longest part of the experience and is often followed by evidence of post-session generalized control efforts in one or more stress-provoking areas of her life not related to food intake.

When feelings of internal control of external events are successfully achieved, they should be accompanied by decreased blood levels of glucocorticoids, epinephrine and norepinephrine. Immediate feelings of success in exercising control appear to be quite reinforcing and should stimulate activity in areas of the brain containing dopaminergic neurons. As discussed earlier in this chapter, such feelings are quite sustaining as they motivate behavior designed to replicate the feelings achieved initially. In the case of CRT, it is typically observed that the patient, prior to encouragement by the therapist, seeks to sustain and regain the feelings achieved in the control reversal experience, which could also account for the early motivation to generalize to other areas of one's life. All sequences of treatment have consisted of no more than 12 sessions of CRT resulting in dramatic changes in the way each patient thinks of herself, her food intake needs, and ways in which she relates to the external entities that previously controlled her life.

A CRT Case Study

An example of a specific case may serve to illuminate the procedure and its effectiveness with anorexic patients. The patient was an attractive sixteen-year-old who was an excellent high school student, an accomplished pianist, and very good at drawing and painting. She reported that despite receiving treatment for her eating disorder in two previous programs, she continued to have obsessive thoughts about ways to control her weight through decreased food intake. She was experiencing increasing feelings of depression, much paranoid ideation concerning friends and acquaintances, and increasing fears about losing her life. Her anorexic behavior had begun before the age of thirteen and her menstrual cycle had never begun despite being only a few weeks from her seventeenth birthday when treatment began.

In her first CRT session, she was asked to help the therapist with a ragtime piano arrangement of Scott Joplin's "The Entertainer" that contained some troublesome fingerings. At first, she reluctantly directed the therapist's efforts which consisted of doing no more than the patient asked, but enough to demonstrate that everything she asked would be attempted. Phase two began after about 15–20 minutes when her instructions abruptly became much more assertive and were accompanied by fingering demonstrations, instructions for practicing techniques, and occasional questions about what the therapist had learned so far. When the nature of her directives had calmed to a point that she seemed satisfied with the therapist's understanding of how to proceed, the therapist thanked her for the assistance in an obvious signal that she had provided sufficient instruction for that session. However, instead of relinquishing control back to the therapist, she acted quickly and decisively to employ a tactic designed to retain control of the session for a longer period of time. Thus began phase three. She directed the therapist to move away from the center of the piano in order for her to demonstrate certain passages that she wanted the therapist to practice in specific ways. It has been found that this type of behavior is typical of patients upon experiencing CRT for the first time.

Each subsequent session began by providing the patient an opportunity to openly discuss any issues of her choosing that may have arisen since the prior session, and continued with music-based procedures such as those described in a) through f) above. Following each experience, the patient was allowed to do a drawing with colored markers while in the room alone and with or without background music. According to art therapists who viewed slides of her artwork at a CRT workshop, her first drawing reflected an extremely regressed personality with strong desires to return to the womb. The piano lesson format was abandoned following the second session which began with her announcement that she had successfully gathered the courage to confront her family with her decision to stop taking piano lessons after more than a decade of individual instruction. The session ended with her production of a drawing which she said depicted the fictional killing of her former piano teacher. Part of her personal history included strong resentment and frustration at being made at an early age to study piano with a very demanding piano teacher.

Other sessions were designed to provide the patient with an opportunity to be in a controlling position while confronting specific issues and relationships that had affected her life. As the series of CRT sessions progressed, her reports continued of additional episodes in which she assumed personal control of events in her life, although she was never told that such changes were the true goal of treatment. She talked more positively about weight gains and about her friends, and her drawings gradually reflected less turmoil in her psychological life. Although these factors were encouraging and her ease at assuming control had improved during sessions, there was no other evidence that her basic illness was subsiding until she arrived for what turned out to be her twelfth and final treatment session. She happily announced that her menstrual cycle had finally begun, which was at that time a few weeks beyond her seventeenth birthday. If true, the therapeutic significance of this event meant that the technique of restoring the patient's perception of control in her life had been successful in achieving the biomedical gains needed to also restore the body's ability to function normally.

CRT Applications

When CRT is effectively administered, the patient will feel much less need to use the eating disorder as a transference mechanism to satisfy her need for internal control of events in her life. The true therapeutic objective is achieved when the patient becomes able to release cortical control of her body's natural processes and allow the endocrine glands to resume regulation of eating and drinking behavior through production of peptide hormones, and the hypothalamus to again assume its ordinary role in controlling food intake by responding to neuropeptide Y and other input.

The key to reversing this disorder had been suggested by reports that ability to exert some control over one's situation reduces the stress response in both animals and humans. "Situations that permit some control are less likely to produce signs of stress than those in which other people (or machines) control the situation" (Carlson, p. 349). It is possible that this technique or a procedure with similar goals may be effective with other types of patients for whom lack of control is an issue, such as victims of abuse or sexual assault and patients suffering from some forms of posttraumatic stress disorder.

BIOMEDICAL INFLUENCES OF MUSIC
ON BEHAVIOR DISORDERS

When interpreting psychiatric music therapy from a biomedical viewpoint, it is important to understand that music does not have the power to simply enter the brain and independently reverse a serious disorder by affecting neurological functions. It does, however, assist the therapist in eliciting certain mood changes and feeling states that allow the patient to exhibit and experience the effects of certain therapeutically beneficial responses. While the music alone does not rehabilitate the patient, it can affect reality contact through sensory stimulation and kinesthetic feedback. It is also used to structure interpersonal interaction and serve as a basis for participation in social groups or society at large. If administered independently of its relationship to the therapist, it may serve to intensify the pathology with which the patient is afflicted.

For example, for those persons exhibiting antisocial personality disorders, certain songs may have the effect of validating pathological thoughts and values. The behaviors resulting from those ideas are often found to provide feelings of reinforcement and self-esteem that were not achieved through more appropriate means. The feelings of reinforcement occur when the brain dispenses sensations of reward through release of endogenous opiates. These opiates stimulate receptors on the membranes of various other neurons. If the behavior disorder involves the intake of nonendogenous opiates (drugs), it stimulates numerous receptors and produces effects such as analgesia, sedation, and reinforcement. The latter effect is due to the effects of opiates on the ventral tegmental area where dopaminergic neurons are activated. Unfortunately, there is substantial evidence suggesting that overactivity of these same neurons is a primary cause of schizophrenia (Carlson, 1992).

When utilized by a therapist the same music that suggests negative images, behaviors, and roles can be used to help the patient examine his or her own role models, values, and personal goals, and to experience the reinforcement that is found through other more productive activities. Open and reasoned discussion of the lyrics of certain music that antisocial individuals listen to, for example, can provide a safe framework within which the person can experience self expression and exploration of the basic values, if any, that tend to drive the antisocial behavior. Certain active playing experiences are effective in helping the person with an antisocial personality disorder combat the impulsive behavior that is used to seek immediate stimulation and gratification. Waiting one's turn to play a handbell or tone chime, for example, forces the patient to make use of frontal lobe structures to overcome deficits in delayed response performance, thereby preventing impulsive behaviors from occurring. The frontal lobes also become occupied with evaluating the consequences of specific actions, a cognitive task not generally associated with the antisocial person (Thompson, 1967).

EPILOGUE

This chapter has examined the biomedical basis of musical influences on human emotion, reinforcement, and emotional cognition. Specific application of such influences in the medical arena and with selected psychiatric clients also was included. Effects of music on the emotional status of each patient also constitute a prominent area of concern when addressing the physical and communication disorders discussed in Chapter 6.

VI

MUSIC FOR RECOVERY OF PHYSICAL AND COMMUNICATION SKILLS

W hen the music therapist engages a patient in an activity that includes making musical sounds rather than only listening to the music, it is important for the therapist to always be cognizant of the role of the brain in the music making process. Whether the musical endeavor is vocal or involves manipulation of a musical instrument or other apparatus, the patient is being asked to move his or her body parts through the conscious use of muscles and muscle groups. In so doing, the musical activity serves as a framework within which the patient's brain must become active in planning movements and sending the needed nerve impulses through efferent motor pathways to the muscles themselves. Without this process, there can be no independent movement and no music will be produced.

The range of possible demands on the motor cortex is very large and can be controlled by the music therapist through the selection of specific instruments to address specific therapeutic objectives. Motor involvement may be limited to the use of one finger which is all that is needed to produce very reinforcing sounds on an omnichord. Activities using keyboard and percussion instruments may be designed to use an entire hand or both hands. Instruments such as the organ and harp can require both hands and feet to play. Wind instruments generally engage both hands along with the musculature of respiration, while singing involves respiratory muscles and the articulators. All such activities utilize cranial areas responsible for both association and motor functions. Specific musical procedures may be designed to use musical cognition and aesthetic experiences to stimulate use and improvement in motor functions. Procedures are designed to use familiar motor activity to enhance cognitive processing or to aid rehabilitation of skills needed for interpersonal communication.

The third Hypothesis of the biomedical theory addresses the importance of the brain in all endeavors involving bodily movement, and consequently its importance in rehabilitation of motor functions in patients:

> Active participation in expressive musical activities provides structured movement behaviors necessary for maintenance or recovery of physical function, and for development of the skills necessary for interpersonal communication.

Selection of music activities to utilize the interdependence of the brain and muscles must be based on a thorough understanding of normal neuromuscular functioning within the human body. The next section is intended to provide basic information about types of muscles, motor neurons, sensors that provide feedback to the brain, and the organization of the motor cortex.

CORTICAL CONTROL OF MOVEMENT
DURING MUSICAL ACTIVITY

In descriptions of her work with nursing home residents, Slabey (1985) included an account of a man who had suffered a leg amputation, an aphasic loss of speech, and loss of ability to use his right arm. Therefore, he no longer used either hand to play his mandolin or banjo. However, with the help of the therapist's right hand to strum the strings, he regained the motivation to use his left hand to finger the chords on the frets. Subsequently, he began to sing familiar lyrics calmly, clearly, and correctly along with the instrumental accompaniment. What aspect of the musical experience motivated this renewed use of his left upper extremity and stimulated rediscovery of his oral verbal capacities? Clearly, it was the ability of the therapist to involve all parts of the person's brain in cognitive, associative, emotional, and motor responses to music that elicited purposeful and effective movement activities in skeletal, respiratory, and articulatory musculature.

Although the use of rhythm and other aspects of musical stimulation to elicit and organize motor behavior can be demonstrated readily, Thaut et al. (1994) stated, "our understanding of the physiological mechanisms involved in this phenomenon is very poor and it is this paucity of scientific knowledge which has contributed to the rather limited acceptance of sensory stimulation in, for example, motor rehabilitation."

MUSCLES AND NEURAL INNERVATION

To understand the motor functions involved in the processes referred to above, it is necessary to know how muscles are stimulated and the difference between various types of muscles. The actions of **skeletal muscles** are the most noticeable because they move fingers, hands, arms, legs, feet, torso, head, neck, and portions of the face. They are connected to bones by tendons and work in opposing, yet cooperating groups of flexors and extensors.

Use of a particular muscle requires that it contract in response to a command issued from the brain. Contracture is accomplished when **extrafusal muscle fibers** are stimulated by activity of **alpha motor neurons**. Feedback of information on muscle contraction to the brain is accomplished by sense organs in muscles called **muscle spindles** that are sensitive to stretch, and that contain small intrafusal muscle fibers that are stimulated by **gamma motor neurons**. Additional feedback is sent to the brain by **Golgi tendon** organs located in the tendons. These sensors measure the amount of force exerted by the muscle on the bone (Carlson, 1992).

When an axon of a motor neuron fires, acetylcholine is released which depolarizes the membrane of the muscle fiber. This depolarization causes calcium channels to open allowing calcium ions to enter and trigger an action potential in the muscle fiber membrane, thereby causing a contraction of the muscle fiber. The strength of the contraction is determined by the firing rate of the motor neurons. This sequence is repeated countless times under direct control of the brain whenever a client plays an instrument, taps a finger or toe, sings a song, or otherwise moves while participating in a musical experience.

Skeletal muscles respond to instructions received from the **primary motor cortex**, which is located on the precentral gyrus just in front of the central sulcus. The amount of motor cortex devoted to each part of the body is directly proportional to the amount of use of each body part. This area directly controls specific movements in accordance with motor planning that is accomplished in the frontal cortex. The frontal association cortex formulates these plans based on immediate sensory data, memories of exteroceptive and somatosensory sensations, and information received from association areas in occipital, temporal and parietal lobes.

A second type of muscle in the human body is **smooth muscle** which is controlled by the autonomic nervous system. This type of muscle is found in large arteries, around hair follicles to produce piloerection, in the eye where it determines pupillary dilation, and in the gastrointestinal system and uterus. A third type of muscle, **cardiac muscle**, has the appearance of skeletal muscle but its contractions are not directed by the brain. Like smooth muscle, its activity can be modulated by neural impulses and by hormones such as epinephrine and norepinephrine. Participation in music, whether playing or just listening, has been shown by numerous investigators to have observable effects on smooth and cardiac muscle activity under some conditions.

CRANIAL PATHWAYS FOR MOTOR RESPONSES TO MUSIC

When a musical activity stimulates the brain to respond with bodily movement, the primary motor cortex has four different pathways through which to exercise control of these movements. The corticospinal pathway contains axons that extend through the medulla to the gray matter of the spinal cord. The temporal and parietal lobes of the brain also send fibers that descend through this pathway. This system includes neurons with cell bodies in the arm and hand region of the primary motor cortex. Its use is essential for independent use of the hands and fingers, such as for playing instruments like the mandolin or banjo.

The corticobulbar pathway also originates in the primary motor cortex and projects to the medulla, but its neurons terminate in motor nuclei of the fifth, seventh, tenth, and twelfth cranial nerves. These projections allow the cortex to control movements of the face and tongue, thereby providing necessary connections to activate and control these muscles during activities such as singing, playing wind instruments, or verbal interaction.

The ventromedial pathways begin in the brain stem and end in the spinal cord gray matter. The three pathways are the vestibulospinal tracts, tectospinal tracts, and reticulospinal tracts located in the brain stem and midbrain reticular formation. In addition to some automatic functions, they control head and trunk movements and their coordination with eye movements. These pathways, therefore, become quite active whenever a person is asked to read music, follow along on a handbell chart, or watch a director for playing cues. Auditory rhythmic signals have been shown to be effective in cuing neuronal activity in motor responses governed by the reticulospinal tract (Thaut et al., 1991).

The fourth pathway is the rubrospinal tract which originates in the red nucleus of the midbrain and sends axons to the spinal cord gray matter. Its primary sources of input are the motor cortex and cerebellum. This tract controls independent movements of the forearms, legs and hands, but does not control muscles of the fingers.

Activities that stimulate use of the four efferent motor pathways described above may generate positive therapeutic gains in head injury clients and others such as those with Rett's Syndrome who exhibit behavioral, psychomotor, and communication impairments. Hadsell and Coleman (1988) reported that basic therapeutic goals with Rett Syndrome clients included promotion of hand usage within structured musical activities, improvement of eye contact, and development of simple communication responses.

CORTICAL CONTROL OF MOTOR ACTIVITY THROUGH RHYTHM

Many authors have asserted the value of rhythm as the operative element in auditory stimulation of cortical activity. This principle has been applied to the use of music to treat a variety of disorders whose performance is dependent upon cerebral cortex functioning. Staum (1983), for example, used **rhythmic auditory stimuli** to facilitate proprioceptive control of rhythmic gait. Subjects attempted to match their footsteps to the sounds of music and other rhythmic percussion sounds. In this study, rhythmic stimuli were faded to promote independence as control increased. All subjects made gains in even walking and/or in maintaining consistency in walking speed.

Thaut et al. (1994) also conducted studies using rhythmic auditory cues to facilitate gait performance in Parkinson's and stroke patients. In subsequent research, rhythmic auditory cuing was used with a forward arm reaching task as an indicator of spatial-temporal organization of sequential movements. Results showed that subjects without auditory cues were not able to perform sequential movements at regular time intervals. However, the use of auditory cuing led to significant decreases in variability of movement duration. Particularly for alternating movements, variability decreases between 30 and 60 percent were observed.

In a separate study, the same researchers compared the effects of rhythmic visual, auditory, and tactile sensory cues on an arm flexion-extension task. Results showed that interval accuracy was significantly greater during auditory cuing than during either visual or tactile cuing even with changing spatial demands. The authors concluded from the two studies that auditory rhythmicity may be important in motor control strategies for spatial-temporal organization of complex, sequential movements in music performance and in music therapy procedures for neuromuscular rehabilitation. Thaut, Schleiffers, and Davis

(1991) offered numerous suggestions for clinical applications of this finding in their report of EMG indications of positive effects of rhythmic auditory stimulation on decreased muscle activity variation, increased duration of muscle activity, improved endurance, and increased coordination in co-contraction of antagonist muscle groups.

MUSIC IN PHYSICAL REHABILITATION

Rehabilitation of individuals with physical disabilities can involve a wide variety of solutions, often ranging from the use of a prosthesis to various forms of electronic assistive technology. The wide variety of available interventions makes it possible to determine which procedures can best be utilized by each person's brain to process motor functions.

Perhaps the most widely known application of music therapy in physical rehabilitation is its use in helping to achieve physical therapy goals. For example, handbell playing has been reported as an effective technique for eliciting an increase in muscle power in the upper extremities of orthopedically impaired children (Itoh & Lee, 1989).

The need to find effective pathways toward rehabilitation is most urgent with clients who have suffered limb **amputations**. Edelstein (1989) has described numerous techniques for adapting playing techniques for unilateral and bilateral amputees, below-elbow and above-elbow, with and without prostheses. Wind, percussion, fretted and unfretted string instruments in acoustic and electrical formats can be incorporated into the rehabilitation program. Alternatives to instrumental participation include composition, conducting, and vocal performance.

Modern computers also provide ample technological assistance for composing, playing back, and imitating the sounds of numerous instruments (Nagler & Lee, 1989). The latter capability is accomplished through the use of Musical Instrument Digital Interface, or MIDI, technology that allows musical sequencers, sound samplers, and signal processing units to be interconnected and to interact through a central computer. MIDI offers the music therapist the opportunity to create a system for specific clients or clinical situations. It has been found to be very useful in work with severely physically impaired clients whose minds and creative potential are still intact.

The need is greatest in the **pediatrics** unit for physical rehabilitation techniques that are motivating and entertaining as well as therapeutically effective. When a child is admitted to a hospital, opportunities for motor involvement may be severely limited by immobilization of all or part of one's body due to various types of illness, trauma, medical procedures, or recovery techniques. Barrickman (1989) used music to facilitate motor development and movement opportunities for children ages 2 to 4 whose physical activity was limited by treatment procedures or medical conditions. Techniques were based on the observation that infants and young children use motor and tactile sensation to test and master the environment. Active musical participation was used to help each child regain some of the pleasure, tension release, and environmental mastery associated with movement during infancy.

Rudenberg and Royka (1989) report that in addition to having positive value in addressing emotional issues, music is used to facilitate range of motion and lung capacity development in children being treated for burns or injuries due to smoke. In work with pediatric burn patients at the Shriners Burn Institute in Galveston, Texas, Rudenberg and Christenberry (1993) observed that many of the children had suffered inhalation injury or had contracted pneumonia. **Respiratory rehabilitation** was initiated with deep breathing exercises during music-assisted relaxation or through the use of simple wind instruments. Recorders and symphonic wind instruments are avoided due to their greater need for digital dexterity and breath control.

The biomedical effect of musical activity in respiratory rehabilitation is to cause the brain to exert conscious control over the otherwise automatic rhythmic discharge emanating from the respiratory center in the medulla. This center normally activates inspiration at moderately paced intervals, unless excessive levels of carbon dioxide (CO_2) or hydrogen ions (H^+) are present to cause changes in the activity of the center (Mader, 1995). It signals the diaphragm to contract with a downward motion and the external intercostal muscles between the ribs to contract moving the rib cage upward and outward. Expiration of air from lungs usually is passive, occurring automatically when the respiratory center stops signalling the diaphragm and external intercostal muscles to contract. The diaphragm presses upward to its relaxed dome shape and the rib cage moves downward and inward, thereby forcing air out of the lungs due to the decreased space. During controlled breathing such as that used to play a wind instrument, the cortex takes over direct control of these muscles by imposing its own timing priorities on the pace and strength of their contractions.

A respiratory illness which, if not controlled, causes a great deal of discomfort to sufferers is asthma. Breathing exercises can help children develop the ability to overcome distress during an attack, although such exercises are unpleasant and repetitious. Fukuda (1993) has described the work of Tateno, a pediatrician who proposed three principles for breathing exercises: 1. If exhalation from chest breathing continues for more than 10 seconds, it will spontaneously switch to abdominal exhalation; 2. loosening abdominal muscles allows abdominal inhalation to occur; 3. the breathing exercises should start with exhalation. A two-part technique was devised to allow children to employ these principles through the more enjoyable practice of singing and blowing wind instruments. "Asthma Music" consisted of singing or playing each line of a familiar song with the addition of a fermata of at least 10 seconds during which the last syllable of the line is held. In the second approach, called the "one-breath" method, children sing or play as much of a song as possible without taking a new breath. This music-based technique is based entirely upon biomedical treatment principles believed necessary for controlling the illness. Excellent results have been reported when the training regimen is adhered to and the abdominal breathing technique is mastered correctly.

MUSIC THERAPY FOR LANGUAGE DISORDERS

To determine the most effective musical procedures for treating language disorders, it is important to understand the normal neurophysiological processes required for language behavior. This section will describe the structures and functions involved in language usage, the neurophysiological basis of certain language disorders that are confronted by music therapists, and specific musical procedures that have been proposed or utilized for treating those disorders.

DISORDERS IN USE OF LANGUAGE SYMBOLS

The extensive use of language symbols in speech and other applications found among the human species is possible only because of the complexity of the human brain. Speech has been referred to as the "single most distinct capability of humans" (Roederer, 1985, p. 83). It involves both expressive and receptive sequencing of auditory symbols, primarily a left hemisphere function, and the recognition and use of vocal inflections, operations that involve the right hemisphere. A speech disorder resulting from damage to the brain is referred to as **aphasia** (Carlson, 1992). Related disorders are apraxia in which a person cannot properly instruct their oral musculature to articulate and produce words due to damage to cortical areas that store motor programming, and dysarthria which is characterized by reduced intelligibility, intensity, and range, and abnormal speaking rates caused by damage to cranial areas that control speech movements (Cohen, 1995).

There are four basic forms of communication that use language symbols. The expressive modes are speaking and writing, and the receptive modes are reading and listening. To accomplish these skills, the brain utilizes sensory pathways in conjunction with one or more of four specialized areas located normally in the left hemisphere. For **listening**, sounds that are perceived in the primary auditory cortex are sent to the rest of the brain. They are picked up by Wernicke's area for processing as auditory word forms. This area is adjacent to the primary auditory area and is responsible for recognizing sounds as words. A lesion in Wernicke's area results in loss of speech comprehension. Patients hear sounds correctly but do not understand spoken language or use the proper words in verbal expression (Taylor, 1989).

For **speaking**, the decision to say a word is passed from cortical association areas to Wernicke's area for formation of the auditory pattern. This information is transmitted through a bundle of axons known as the arcuate fasciculus to Broca's area located adjacent to the left premotor region, the part of the brain that controls speech musculature. Broca's area itself contains stored memory of muscle movement sequences necessary for articulation of words. Its information is shared with both the left and right hemisphere motor areas via the corpus callosum. Lesions in and around Broca's area produce three types of speech deficits in varying amounts in each patient: agrammatism in which there is difficulty in forming grammatical constructions, anomia resulting in an inability to find the desired word, and articulation difficulty in which words are mispronounced by altering the sequence of sounds. Damage to the arcuate fasciculus is a form of conduction aphasia and results in inability to repeat unfamiliar words out loud.

For **reading**, the primary visual cortex sends information to the left angular gyrus located posterior to Wernicke's area. There the stimulus is converted for use by Wernicke's area. Once the auditory form of the word is recognized, it is relayed from Wernicke's area to cortical association areas for speech comprehension. The auditory pattern of a word that is to be read aloud is also sent through the arcuate fasciculus to Broca's area for processing as described above. It should be noted that stimuli in the left visual field are received in the right visual cortex and reach the left angular gyrus via the splenium, a portion of the corpus callosum. Splenium damage results in inability to comprehend written words or describe objects, words, or events localized in the left visual field. Left angular gyrus damage results in a condition known as alexia with agraphia by separating auditory and visual areas of the brain and reducing written words to patterns without auditory forms or meanings to be comprehended (Taylor, 1989). The person can neither read nor write.

Writing behavior requires use of all areas mentioned for the other three skills. A word conceptualized in cortical association areas is recalled in auditory form in Wernicke's area. It is then transmitted via the angular gyrus to the visual association cortex for recall of its written form. This data is sent back through the system to Broca's area for determination of digital musculature coordination and subsequent transmission to the adjacent motor area for control of writing movements. Agraphia can result from damage to any of the specialized speech areas as well as to the visual cortex.

While very noticeable speaking difficulties can be detected when listening to aphasic persons, they exhibit normal use of rhythm, tone, emphasis, and melodic contour as expressive tools. These elements are collectively known as prosody and are common components also of musical expression. This observation strongly suggests that while areas of the brain found most active during speech are different from those activated during musical expression, the use of prosody may engage the same cranial areas for both behaviors. Evidence generally indicates that prosody is a special function of the right cerebral hemisphere (Carlson, 1992). Localization of prosodic functions has allowed development of techniques involving prosody in music as a treatment or training device for improving speech. Rhythm, for example, has become such an important factor in speech training for the deaf that initial emphasis on rhythm followed by stress articulation is considered an appropriate training sequence (Darrow, 1984).

A NEUROPHYSIOLOGICAL MODEL FOR MUSICAL TREATMENT OF APHASIA

Despite the inherent presence of damaged brain tissue in all forms of aphasia, the functional plasticity of the central nervous system has allowed many aphasic disorders to be entirely overcome or helped to some degree. What appears to be occurring is a process in which undamaged neural tissue acts to assume the functions that were normally handled by the damaged area. Some patients exhibit disorders that are much less severe than would be indicated by the nature of cortical damage, some show less aphasic disorder over time, and some recover completely from lesions that usually lead to permanent aphasic disability (Geschwind, 1972). Patients are also observed whose speech is very severely impaired who can sing a melody with words correctly and rapidly while employing prosodic elements for expression.

A neurophysiological model for using music to treat aphasia has been proposed based on the concept of unitary brain functioning and hololisting information processing (Taylor, 1989). This model uses music to enlist the music-related skills of the right cerebral hemisphere to help regain similar speech-related functions lost due to left hemisphere damage. According to this model, the accepted fact that singing can be regained despite left hemisphere damage indicates that use of the right hemisphere in verbal singing activities may assist in regaining some speech capacity when the left hemisphere is damaged. Right hemisphere superiority for melodic and harmonic perception suggests that directed listening experiences may help regain comprehension of spoken language that is lost with damage to Wernicke's area.

Auditory and visual pattern discrimination functions that are the responsibility of the right hemisphere are used for reading both speech and musical notation. Reading and singing music, reading music and playing an instrument, or writing musical notation may be found to be useful procedures for using the right hemisphere to overcome aphasic losses in reading or writing ability.

Singing has long been considered a beneficial form of therapy for persons with aphasic disorders. The behaviors necessary for correct singing, such as proper breathing, phonation, and accuracy in diction, are also essential for intelligible speech (Cohen, 1995). Singing can also provide a rhythmic foundation to help improve verbal expression in aphasic clients (Claeys et al., 1989).

One technique that has received much attention in speech rehabilitation work with aphasics is Melodic Intonation Therapy (MIT). This procedure includes both imitative and responsive singing and is based on the belief that functions associated with the intact right cerebral hemisphere may be used to assist in speech rehabilitation with persons having damage to the left hemisphere (Albert, et al., 1973). MIT was used in a study of five male patients who had experienced cardiovascular accidents, two of whom were diagnosed with global aphasia, two exhibited mixed aphasia, and one had Broca's aphasia (Laughlin, et al., 1979). The investigators believed that aphasic patients with damage to the left hemisphere and auditory processing disorders would benefit from extended duration of both verbal and nonverbal auditory stimuli. Performance of subjects was compared using 1.5 and 2.0 second syllable durations. All subjects were found to have the highest number of correct phrase productions with the 2.0 second syllable duration, next highest with 1.5 second syllables, and the lowest number with nonintoned regular speech. These findings appear to indicate that music therapists should use slower tempos along with slowed conversational speech when working with aphasic patients.

Cohen (1995) used breathing instruction, vocal exercises, and singing in attempting to *in*crease speaking rates by decreasing pause times of two aphasic clients who had been diagnosed with dysarthria. She also sought to gain improvements in their vocal intensity, frequency range, and verbal intelligibility. The two subjects experienced 38% and 11% reductions in pause time, and one increased 11% in verbal intelligibility. Frequency range during speaking did not change for either subject.

Most investigations of the effects of music on the speech of brain injured subjects has focused on those with left hemisphere damage. Cohen (1988) used rhythm to help *de*crease the rate of speech of an 18-year-old adolescent girl who had experienced a partial right hemisphere craniotomy (removal) and additional injury to the temporal-parietal lobes. The subject exhibited dysarthria and multiple disorders in nonspeech areas of behavior, although her musical abilities were unimpaired. Music at 80 beats per minute and a matching tapping movement were used as pacing devices to slow the subject's rate of speech. An 11% decrease in speaking rate was achieved, and a 28% decrease from the original baseline was obtained using a rhythmic variable without melody.

SENSORY DISORDERS:
ENHANCING COMMUNICATION SKILLS WITH MUSIC

With many clients, their language problems can be attributed to sensory disorders that have taken away normal receptive communication modes and necessitated adjustments in expressive behaviors. These disorders generally have a physical or neurophysiological cause that is clearly identifiable and which leads to impairment in development of communication skills. Whether the disorder is due to a problem of the sensory organ itself, the peripheral nerves that carry sensory information to the central nervous system, or the neural structures that decode incoming sensory impulses and realize them as actual sensations, the problem is ultimately one in which the brain does not receive the kind of exteroceptive data or proprioceptive feedback needed to function normally. In order to plan musical interventions aimed at improving the communication skills of these populations, it is important to understand the physiological etiology and related factors confronted by individuals with sensory disorders.

Kersten (1989) has written a detailed review of the definitions, causality, and importance of musical involvement for visually impaired individuals. Five separate definitions are provided with corresponding numerical visual acuity ranges specified. In discussing the physiological importance of musical participation, the author stresses rhythm as a basis for movement to bring about enrichment in the intellectual life of the visually impaired person. Underutilized muscles and muscle groups are stimulated through motor activity during musical experiences with resulting enhancement of motor development. Rhythmic exercises also promote physical coordination in children whose awkward carriage often draws attention to their disability. Music also assists in achieving needed relaxation of the tension that accrues due to inactivity, lack of emotional expression, and excessive concentration needed to accomplish each task.

Some musical instruments afford a release of the anger that is otherwise dissipated through stereotypical mannerisms associated with blindness. Psychological energy often generated within emotional centers in the brain cannot be vented upon an object when one cannot be located through visual means. Within musical participation, the nonsighted individual can function on an equal basis with his or her sighted peers, which can be quite reinforcing and can provide corresponding benefits to that person's brain (The biomedical basis of reinforcement was discussed in the preceding chapter). Certain skills specific to the blind, such as reading and writing braille, can also be practiced through the use of braille sheet music.

A substantial amount of computer-based technology continues to appear to assist those with visual impairments in receiving environmental feedback and in expressing themselves in a variety of ways. These include braille keyboards, converters that translate braille and conventional print for instant communication, speech synthesis devices for voice renditions of computer programs, and high-speed braille printers. Devices of this type give the nonsighted person greater access and control of the environment. Therapists should consider using such forms of assistive technology to help visually impaired clients achieve the benefits of song- writing, composing, and numerous other applications available to their sighted peers in music therapy.

Darrow, Gfeller (1984, 1991, 1991) and others have described and investigated the benefits and applications of music with hearing impaired children. Music therapists should be cognizant of the type and amount of hearing impairment experienced by each client or student before planning adaptations or expressive musical activities. Types of hearing impairments are identified by the location of the source of the problem and the severity of hearing loss, although knowledge of the location is of little value to the music therapist. The ultimate goal of the therapist is to help the client receive as much as possible of the information that would normally arrive via auditory sensation, and use that input in effectively responding to the environment.

Music therapy activities can help the brain of the hearing impaired client learn to develop and use skills related to language such as rhythm, pace, dynamics, tone quality, pitch control, and muscular coordination. Movement activities, vocal pitch matching, song lyric signing, instrumental music, and songwriting are some of the techniques that can help develop the vestibular, motor, cognitive, emotional, expressive, and receptive sensory capacities of the hearing impaired client's brain. Building upon these elements, many hearing impaired persons gain or regain full use of their speaking abilities.

MUSIC MEDICINE: TREATMENT FOR INJURED MUSICIANS

Development of musical skill involves complex interactions between the nervous system, musculoskeletal system, respiratory apparatus, and sense organs working together to produce music. When any one system experiences a health problem, it interferes with the entire process of musical development (Manchester, 1988). In the central nervous system, the brain is so essential to the operation and coordination of musical behavior that problems in key cortical structures can entirely disable an individual's musical endeavors. In the musculoskeletal system, nerve innervation of skeletal muscles, contraction capabilities of the muscles themselves, and the strength of bones and connective tissue all play essential roles in maintaining the ability to produce music. Similar conclusions can be drawn concerning the importance of maintaining adequate capability in vocal, respiratory, and auditory systems.

Despite awareness of the need to avoid incorrect use or overuse of one's body in pursuing musical excellence, the need to continue to practice and perform is also essential—especially for the career musician. In the field of music medicine, studies are being undertaken to determine the incidence of performance related injuries and the most effective ways to prevent or treat those injuries. Medical concerns relating to injuries experienced by musicians include pain and loss of function in working structures of the body, occupational stress, the musical environment, and access to therapeutic intervention when problems occur. International studies show that injuries occur in up to 20% of music students and over 50% of orchestral performers (Lee & Kella, 1989). Problems include nerve compression syndromes, muscular and tendon disorders, dermatitis, dental and other oral problems, cardiac irregularities, and miscellaneous problems of the eyes, respiratory apparatus, and vocal chords. Diagnostic procedures include direct observation via arthroscopic surgery, x-ray photography, electrodiagnostics such as electromyography, and computerized thermography. The latter technique measures changes in body temperature or differences in heat emission patterns as indicators of metabolic activity, changes in peripheral blood flow, or altered sympathetic nerve function.

An important component in music medicine is the potential gain from preparing music educators in the basic anatomy and physiology of each of their performance areas. It is helpful for the performing arts medical specialist to become knowledgeable of the physical requirements for playing specific instruments and singing. However, if the music teacher is aware of potential problems and solutions, many disabilities may be prevented or corrected before they reach the doctor's office (Manchester, 1988).

There is no one method of prevention or intervention that is agreed upon by all practitioners of music medicine. Fry (1989) has asserted that the occurrence of a medical condition in a musician may result from the condition being imitated by a more common condition called overuse injury syndrome. This syndrome results from excessive or unaccustomed use of muscles and joints and is manifested as a primary condition of pain or loss of function. Factors leading to overuse injury syndrome are intense use over time, individual playing technique, and individual susceptibility. Changes in practicing or performing demands or adoption of new techniques when studying with a new teacher may bring about the appearance of the syndrome. Noteworthy examples that often generate both situations occur when a child goes away to music camp, and when a performer acquires a professional performing position in an orchestra that has long daily performances and rehearsals. Both events take the performer away from home and may require extended playing under new teachers and conductors.

Perhaps the most damaging injury that can be experienced by a musician would be damage to the brain that results in a condition known as amusia. Amusia is a loss of musical ability and results from brain lesions that may be initiated by trauma or by an illness that attacks the neurological system. In a study of the frequency and type of amusia associated with various cerebral lesions, Oepen and Berthold (1985) studied 34 subjects, 16 of whom exhibited aphasia, and 12 of whom showed amusia without aphasia. All subjects had musical training and/or experience. Results indicated that receptive amusia was more severe in left hemisphere subjects with a close relationship between receptive rhythm problems and aphasia. Rhythm losses were especially severe in left hemisphere subjects. Subjects with right hemisphere damage showed a greater frequency of expressive rhythmic and melodic disturbances. General musical ability disturbances were more frequently observed in musicians after left hemisphere accidents. It was reported that the language of aphasic subjects did not improve during singing, a condition which would be expected with subjects also suffering from amusia.

An important issue in the health of performing musicians is that of performance anxiety. This phenomenon is experienced to some degree at all levels of musical development. Mental and physical manifestations can range from very minor to so severe that it becomes impossible to perform successfully. Most procedures for addressing performance related anxiety and tension are primarily cognitive and may be accompanied by other more overtly observable devices. Montello (1992) has researched this topic at length and has provided a variety of techniques for confronting the problem.

An area of great concern to the music medicine specialist is the musical environment. Many musicians have experienced damage to their auditory systems from elevated decibel levels used by groups in which they perform. The listener in the audience may also be subject to cochlear damage while too close to an electronic amplification device or while using earphones with a portable personal electronic music system. Increased public awareness of the dangers of heightened decibel levels and availability of corrective resources is needed as part of the preventive effort being supported by music medicine practitioners.

VII

MUSICAL INFLUENCES ON ANXIETY AND STRESS PHYSIOLOGY

H istorically, the most widely accepted application of music as a therapeutic agent is its use as a calming agent to combat anxiety, tension, and stress. The need to appropriately manage stress is easily understood through the many widely recognized effects of excess stress on human health and behavior. These effects include the development of physical problems such as hypertension, ulcers, skin disorders, headaches, arteriosclerosis, reproductive dysfunctions, coronary disease, respiratory ailments, and changes in lymphocyte levels that increase the risk of cancer. Also associated with anxiety and stress are fluid retention, obesity, psychosomatic symptoms, and increased rates of depression and suicide (Hanser, 1985).

Perhaps because of the many physiological changes that attend these states, anxiety has come to be identified by its numerous associated physiological changes including such parameters as heart rate, blood pressure, galvanic skin response, and electromyographic and electroencephalographic responses. One method that individuals use to cope with anxiety or stress is to attempt to confront or remove the stress-provoking source. Otherwise, they may attempt to manage it in specific situations through relaxation, a method designed to keep their own emotions from interfering with their ability to function effectively as well as to minimize the effects of associated physiological changes that could occur.

Wide use of the terms anxiety, tension, and stress in both conversational and research language has made their meanings controversial and their differences unclear (Hanser, 1985). Those who write professional literature on the topic of anxiety have adopted the terms "state anxiety" to refer to a temporary state of fear of one's own ability to cope successfully with the threats or demands of a given situation (also referred to as "situational anxiety"), and "trait anxiety" to refer to a more permanent state of uneasiness resulting from a general awareness or belief in one's own lack of well-being.

For purposes of the following discussion, the terms shall not be used interchangeably. Semantic differentiation can be readily achieved by recognizing that the three terms may be used to refer to three different temporal positions in relationship to the stress-provoking event. Anxiety is used herein to refer to feelings of fear and associated discomfort resulting from awareness of a future event that may present a threat or set of demands that the individual feels ill prepared to deal with successfully. Tension shall refer to those feelings of uneasiness or inadequacy that occur *during* the event or while in the presence of the threatening object. It is recognized, however, that the concept of tension has physiological applications that may accurately describe one's functioning status during periods of anxiety or stress. Stress will be used to designate the more continuous reactions that may not be related to a single event or object, but which may persist due to ongoing perception of aversive or threatening situations or to unresolved conflicts in the recent or distant past.

With the above definitions in mind, the fourth and final Hypothesis of the Biomedical Theory of Music Therapy may be stated as follows:

Music has a direct effect on specific physiological processes whose functional variations are indicators of anxiety, tension or stress.

The quest for a basis upon which to build musical interventions for calming anxious listeners began in earnest during the 1950s. Many investigators believed that they could listen to a selection of music and categorize it as "stimulative" or "sedative" before observing its effect on listeners. A major contributor to this belief was the use of a pair of definitions offered by Gaston in 1951. Those definitions read as follows:

Stimulative music enhances bodily energy, induces bodily action, stimulates the striped muscles, the emotions and subcortical reactions of man, and is based on such elements as strong rhythms, volume, cacophony, and detached notes....

Sedative music is of a sustained melodic nature, with strong rhythmic and percussive elements largely lacking. This results in physical sedation, and responses of an intellectual and contemplative nature rather than physical. (p. 143)

In using these descriptions, most investigators based the process of classification on the properties of the music and chose to ignore the portion of each definition that described the effects on listeners. Consequently, other variables that often influence the responses of listeners were not accounted for prior to labeling each selection. Subsequent research using galvanic skin response and questionnaire data showed that when precategorizations were tested against actual responses, the subjects did not respond in accordance with the stimulative or sedative preclassifications assigned to the music by the investigators (Taylor, 1973). It has therefore become necessary to play a potentially sedating selection for a patient or subject before determining which music will have a calming effect during periods of anxiety.

PHYSIOLOGY OF ANXIETY AND STRESS

To understand the effects of music on the physiology of anxiety and stress, it is necessary to more closely examine parts of the limbic system and their relationship to hormonal secretions from the endocrine glands. Studies show that the central nucleus of the amygdala sends projections to parts of the brain that react to aversive stimuli. These include portions of the lower brain stem that are involved in controlling the autonomic nervous system and a nucleus in the hypothalamus that is active in the secretion of stress-related hormones. When the perception of an aversive situation results in stimulation of the central nucleus of the amygdala, there are resulting increases in heart rate and blood pressure which contribute to the awareness of physiological changes during anxiety. Carlson (1992) has shown that gastric ulcers may be produced if stimulation is long-term. It follows, therefore, that the autonomic responses controlled by the central nucleus of the amygdala can be causally related to the harmful effects of long-term stress, such as circulatory, coronary, and gastric problems.

The amygdala is also involved in organizing behavioral responses to emotions such as anger and its behavioral correlate aggression. It also mediates fear reactions which result in defensive responses. It is important to consider that both anger and fear are object-related emotions. An individual feels anger at, and fear of, something or someone. Like fear, anxiety also is an emotional response to specific internal and external stimuli. It contains all of the same elements of the fear emotion except that it is not directed toward immediate action or thought that would remove the effect of the stimulus (Birbaumer, 1983). When responses to the object of one's anger or fear continue over an extended period of time without resolution or reduction of the anger or fear, the neurophysiological responses that constitute these feelings also persist, often with serious harmful effects such as high blood pressure due to pro-longed stimulation of the central nucleus of the amygdala. Traditional ways of treating such stress-related disorders have included administering barbiturates or antianxiety drugs. Before examining music as a stress abatement technique, it is important to review both the helpful and harmful effects of pharmacologi-cal interventions.

STRESS PHARMACOLOGY AND MUSICAL INTERVENTION

Barbiturates affect the brain by depressing its activity, in part by increas-ing GABA (gamma-aminobutyric acid) receptor sensitivity. GABA is an amino acid neurotransmitter which acts to keep nerve impulses from spreading ran-domly throughout the brain to neurons other than the target neurons at the synapse. When such random uncontrolled nerve firing throughout the brain does occur, it is called a "seizure." By allowing brain cells to be more receptive to GABA, low doses of barbiturates slow down neuronal activity sufficiently to result in a calming or sedative response. When abused by people seeking to counteract feelings of anxiety, slightly higher doses of barbiturates can produce motor discoordination, unconsciousness, coma or even a fatal depression of the respiratory centers of the medulla. Alcohol has similar effects on brain cell ac-tivity and results in similar problems when used in increasingly larger doses (Carlson, 1992). These risks may be avoided by using musical impulses instead of barbiturates or alcohol to slow brain activity. If GABA receptivity is low, thereby increasing the likelihood of random impulse spread, musical activity may be used to synchronize neuronal discharge patterns in such a way that any abnormal spread of nerve impulses will be incorporated into the musical task.

Antianxiety drugs are traditionally classified as benzodiazepines. These substances activate sites on receptor nerves that cause GABA to be even more effective in inhibiting the ability of neurotransmitter-dependent ion channels to initiate a nerve impulse in the receptor neuron. Benzodiazepines are effective in treating anxiety disorders and insomnia. It has been found, however, that dependence on sleep medications is the most common cause of insomnia in the United States (Carlson, 1992). The reason is that benzodiazepines, for example, cause "rebound" insomnia when their effect wears off after a certain amount of time. Therefore, they should be used only as short-term treatment for insomnia, although they are sometimes inappropriately used by patients or prescribed by doctors over a longer period of time.

Stress refers to the physiological reaction caused by the continuous perception of threatening situations. The perception of such threats generates a sustained stress reaction in which the adrenal glands secrete epinephrine which affects glucose metabolism, norepinephrine that increases heart output and blood pressure, and steroid stress hormones such as cortisol. Research has shown however, that music significantly reduces pulse rate and plasma levels of epinephrine, norepinephrine, and cortisol in patients undergoing medical and dental procedures (Spintge & Droh, 1987).

Cortisol is a glucocorticoid that serves to conserve blood glucose by profoundly affecting glucose metabolism, helping break down protein and converting it to glucose, and increasing blood flow. Sustained stress results in prolonged secretion of glucocorticoids with long-term effects such as high blood pressure, increased risk of heart attacks and strokes, steroid diabetes, infertility, inhibition of the inflammatory response, and suppression of the immune system. Research has shown that prolonged exposure to glucocorticoids destroys neurons in part of the hippocampus by increasing their susceptibility to events such as decreased blood flow, and by lowering their ability to utilize glucose. As blood flow decreases, the insufficient metabolic activity causes the neurons to die (Carlson, 1992).

In addition to the extended situations that elicit stress reactions, immediate occurrences can cause an increase in pituitary ACTH (adrenocorticotropic hormone) which controls the secretion of cortisol by the adrenal cortex. The largest hormonal increases occur with presentation of aversive events that are either completely unpredictable or completely predictable (Birbaumer, 1983).

In studying the effects of music on various parameters of anxiety and stress physiology, Miluk-Kolasa (1993) reported that emotions are a manifestation of limbic system functioning status, and that limbic system functioning may be modified by the cerebral cortex. Music, which gains access to the body only through the cerebral cortex, is known to elicit emotions. In her research music material was selected by individually interviewing every patient in order to determine personal music preferences. During testing, average levels of both cortisol and blood glucose increased in both music and no music presurgical groups upon presentation of a stressor such as information on the time of surgery. Within the group listening to music, blood glucose and cortisol levels rapidly decreased to a point that averaged lower than the original readings. However, cortisol and glucose levels in the no music group increased and remained elevated. These results were obtained using the totally noninvasive method of music treatment, making this intervention particularly attractive.

IMMUNE SYSTEM BIOLOGY AND MUSICAL INFLUENCES

Numerous clinical reports and many research studies have demonstrated a relationship between stress and increased susceptibility to infections due to decreased activity of the immune system. Stress is known to increase secretion of substances that directly suppress immune system activity. Numerous studies have reported that immune responses can be altered through both classical and operant conditioning, and cognitive-behavioral techniques such as hypnosis, progressive muscle relaxation, verbal rehearsal, psychotherapy and mental imagery, although the mechanism for the effect of imagery remains unclear (Rider, 1985).

A more detailed look at musical influences on biological structures and their relationship to immune system function suggests that *music alone* has independent influences on those structures that control this system. In order to understand these effects, it is necessary to first have a good working knowledge of normal immune system functioning. The purpose of the present section is to provide a background for that working knowledge.

The immune system works through the production of white blood cells, all of which have glucocorticoid receptors that appear to mediate immunosuppression during extended periods of stress when the adrenal glands are secreting above normal amounts of cortisol. White blood cells normally protect the body from invasion by bacteria, fungi, and viruses. These cells function as phagocytes and killer cells. Phagocytic white cells operate at the site of an inflammation to destroy both invading cells and debris from the breakdown of the body's own cells. If the invader is a virus, the cell produces a peptide called interferon which inhibits the ability of the virus to reproduce. Natural killer cells are white cells that patrol tissue engulfing and destroying any cell that has become infected by a virus or transformed into a cancer cell. The immune system also includes antibodies, proteins that learn to recognize foreign material known as antigens which mark microbes and other substances for immune system destruction.

Between 40% and 70% of all white cells are neutrophils which phagocytize primarily bacteria. Some white cells that develop in bone marrow are known as B-lymphocytes and release antibodies called immunoglobulins that bind with antigens. In many cases, the foreign material will be phagocytized and destroyed. T-lymphocyte cells are also produced in bone marrow but develop in the thymus gland. They aid the immune system as helper T cells which undergo expansion into suppressor T cells and memory T cells. Once any of these cells recognizes an antigen it will destroy any cell that is bearing that same antigen. Memory T cells remain in blood tissue long after the infection has disappeared and will continue to kill any invader bearing that same antigen. Helper T cells also secrete lymphokines that signal other white blood cells to come and kill the invader. When the antigen is detected by white cells known as monocytes, each of these cells can be activated by lymphocyte products and become a macrophage which kills some bacteria, fungi, and viruses. Macrophages also process antigens for presentation to helper T cells.

Although highly effective under normal circumstances the system breaks down if a corticosteroid such as cortisol is present. It will be detected by the glucocorticoid receptors in white cells, bind with regulatory genes in the cells, and act to block secretion of lymphokines, thereby inhibiting activation of this important signalling mechanism for stimulating additional T cells and other immune cells to respond to an infection.

The immune system may sometimes react to endogenous proteins as antigens and begin to attack noninfected tissue. Such occurrences are called autoimmune diseases, and are exemplified by rheumatoid arthritis and multiple sclerosis (Carlson, 1992; Mader, 1995).

To determine whether music listening would produce changes in the immune system, Bartlett et al. (1993) measured the presence of interleukin-1 (IL-1) and cortisol in blood samples taken from thirty-six experimental and control subjects before and after treatment. IL-1 is identified by the authors as a polypeptide hormone that exists in high concentration in the brain. It is said to be a key mediator in immunological reactions and affects the hypothalamus, promoting secretion of CRF (corticotropin releasing factor) and ACTH stimulation. In this study, subjects were allowed to listen to music that each selected from excerpts of compositions that were considered capable of generating positive listening experiences and relaxation. Seventeen of the eighteen experimental group subjects showed decreased cortisol levels. Analysis of the data showed significant cortisol decreases between pretest and posttest blood samples in the two experimental groups. There was a positive, although inverse, finding for IL-1 with one of the two experimental groups reflecting a significant increase in this substance. The second group and the control group showed no significant differences in IL-1 readings. The significant increase can be understood as an expected desirable result because IL-1 is produced by macrophages and by helper T-cells during periods of infection. It serves as a lymphokine to activate other agents such as cytotropic T cells that destroy cancer cells (Mader, 1995). Its increase in conjunction with significantly decreased cortisol provides strong support for the effectiveness of music in generating immune system recovery.

How, then, does music help restore effective functioning in the immune system? As discussed above, activity in the amygdala is essential in the awareness and expression of mood and emotions. The amygdala receives direct stimulation from the medial division of the medial geniculate nucleus in the thalamus as musical and other auditory stimuli pass through this final relay station in the sound path to the auditory cortex. Consequently, both the amygdala and the hypothalamus, two extremely important control centers for emotion, are beginning to respond to music even before the sound reaches the primary auditory cortex. As the activity levels of neurons in the central nucleus of the amygdala decrease in response to the calming effects of musically stimulated impulses, there are corresponding reductions in the signals being sent out through its projections to other parts of the brain that respond to aversive situations, such as the hypothalamus. The hypothalamus in turn reduces its level of stimulation of the pituitary and endocrine glands, including the adrenal medulla which secretes epinephrine and norepinephrine, and the adrenal cortex which secretes cortisol, a steroid stress hormone. Cortisol belongs to a group of steroids called glucocorticoids, some of which are known to cause significant decreases in the number of T-cells in circulation, thereby decreasing the potency of the immune response. With less cortisol to impair white blood cell activity, the immune system is free to recover its normal function of attacking invading cells.

The brain is responsible for immunosuppression through its control of pituitary secretion of ACTH which mediates secretion of glucocorticoids. "The most important mechanism by which stress impairs immune function is the increased blood levels of glucocorticoids" (Carlson, 1992, p. 355). In short, music can calm neural activity in the brain, resulting in decreased glucocorticoid production and associated recovery of normal white blood cell activity.

MANAGING ANXIETY AND STRESS
IN INFANTS AND CHILDREN

In the sixth century, Boethius noted that music could affect moral development, and that the physiological effects of music on infants were different when "contrasting the calming effects of a lullaby with the excitation of a 'shrill and harsh' melody" (Pratt, 1989, p. 3). Current research using lullabies and other vocal children's music suggests that music played in a Newborn ICU may have significantly reduced initial weight loss, increased daily average weight, increased formula and caloric intake, and reduced both length of stay and the average daily occurrence of "stress behaviors" (Caine, 1991).

Reducing tension and stress-related responses in newborn infants takes on added importance when the baby is premature. Staff at a large hospital in central Wisconsin believe that the use of music may have lifesaving significance in their attempts to give premature babies a better chance to survive. It is believed that the music helps them breathe more easily, remain more relaxed physically, and experience improved oxygenation. Premature babies who may be under stress from an underdeveloped breathing apparatus and who may have other illnesses tend to indulge in hypertensive motor behaviors, such as kicking and screaming, which uses up oxygen faster than it can be utilized by the body. The selected music is soft, gentle, and rhythmic, such as classical music or lullabies. Parents often bring or send taped music especially for times when they cannot be there in person. According to Cook (1981), such music provides sensory stimulation for the baby. She reports that infants who receive appropriate auditory stimuli tend to cry less and gain weight more rapidly.

Chetta (1981) reported work showing that even minor procedures can evoke an adrenocortical response. This finding implies the need to reduce anxiety and stress in hospitalized children. To determine the effect of music on anxiety and fear behaviors during induction of preoperative medication, she studied the responses of 75 pediatric surgical patients between 3 and 8 years of age. The children were divided into three groups. The control group received verbal preoperative instruction the night before surgery. An experimental group received the same verbal instructions on the night prior to surgery except that following the instructions, songs were sung that reviewed the same information and patients were invited to give a doll a shot of make-believe medication. A second experimental group received the same music-based preparation on the night before surgery and more music immediately before induction of preoperative medication on the morning of the surgery. Results indicated that the group that received music therapy in the morning just before induction of preoperative medication was rated as exhibiting significantly less anxiety than both of the other two groups. Anxiety ratings between the control group and the group receiving instructions with music therapy the night before surgery were not significantly different. The investigator concluded that the presence of the music therapist at the time of preoperative medication induction seemed of great value in emotionally preparing the child for the induction procedure.

ANXIOLYTIC MUSIC IN MEDICAL AND DENTAL PROCEDURES

Spintge and Droh (1992) have stated their belief that no behavior is without emotion. They also observed that research in neurophysiology demonstrates effective and therapeutic influences of music on all modalities of emotional expression. In their surgical practice, they have created applications in which they perioperatively utilized a multimodal system to monitor emotional and therapeutic effects of music. A primary advantage of the system is that they can remain informed of the effects of music on the patient's state of anxiety according to neurophysiological indicators. The music, called anxiolytic music, is noninvasive, nondisruptive of medical procedures, and the system allows telemetric monitoring during active music therapy. Anxiolytic music can be described as any music that has the effect of reducing anxiety.

The multimodal system consists of observation and analysis of verbal content, cognitive-verbal behavior assessment via psychological tests, monitoring of peripheral parameters such as pulse rate, blood pressure, EKG, heart and respiratory rate, skin temperature, oxygen consumption, and CO^2 production. Central nervous system monitoring includes parameters such as blood levels of beta-endorphin and ACTH. Nonverbal psychomotor behaviors such as facial expressions, fight-flight reactions, and nail biting are observed and analyzed. Questionnaires and interviews also are employed to evaluate situational subjective feelings before, during, and after treatment.

The multimodal monitoring system has been applied in surgery, obstetrics, and dental treatment. In surgery, anxiety among music patients dropped from 70% before the operation to 20% perioperatively, compared to a drop to 40% for the control group.

There were no fight-flight reactions among music groups in any of the studies. Of these 75,000 patients, 95% confirmed that music had an anxiolytic effect, bringing calm and relieving anxiety and distress. A very important result observed throughout the series of studies was that the use of anxiolytic music led to a 50% reduction in use of sedative, analgesic and anesthetic drugs compared to the usual dosage.

In the abstract of his presentation to a 1994 symposium on music in medicine, Dr. Fred Schwartz, an anesthesiologist from Atlanta, Georgia, reported his observations of the use of music in the operating room as well as in the preoperative stage. He asserted that there is "no doubt" that the presurgical time is filled with anxiety and fear of loss of control, negative outcome, and pain. He described the role of the sympathetic nervous system (SNS) in mediating many of the harmful effects of stress during an operation, such as production of the catecholamines dopamine, epinephrine, and norepinephrine. Certain body functions such as heart rate and blood pressure are increased, a condition which can lead to ischemia or myocardial infarction for the patient with significant coronary disease.

Dr. Schwartz reported that music had been found to have numerous beneficial effects in dental and surgical applications. Among these are its effects on emotions via the limbic and hypothalamic brain structures, the SNS, and on production of stress hormones. During dental procedures, use of music was found to result in heart rate and blood pressure changes, and in lower levels of the stress hormones ACTH, prolactin, and growth hormone (HGH). In surgery, the rise in cortisol was decreased with the effect continuing in the recovery room in the absence of music. Under regional or local anesthesia, systolic and diastolic blood pressure and respiratory rates were lower with music. Music masked or distracted the patient from operating room sounds and conversations, helped put some patients to sleep even without general anesthesia, lowered the time needed to complete some procedures, and facilitated a more pleasant and harmonious working environment by decreasing levels of frustration and fatigue among surgical staff. It was emphasized that the music must be chosen by the patient for best results.

Background music has been investigated for its anxiolytic effects on patients during surgical operations under epidural anaesthesia. In one study, thirty patients were divided into music and no-music groups for examination of their reactions during operations such as total hip replacement, knee arthroscopy, and abdominal prostatectomy. During epidural anaesthesia, patients can remain awake, alert, and quite aware of their surroundings, although there is no sensation in the physical area of the procedure. Surgical staff had observed that patient preoperative and perioperative anxiety was intensified by the noises and voices of personnel in the operating room. Patients in the experimental group listened to music that they selected. It was played through headphones from immediately after the start of epidural anaesthesia until the operation was completed. Control group subjects had no headphones or music. Plasma levels of such stress indicators as ACTH, cortisol, and the catecholamines were monitored from blood samples drawn periodically during the procedures. Analysis of results did not find significant differences in plasma hormone levels, heart rate, or mean arterial blood pressure between the two groups. However, it was shown that while plasma levels of all hormones increased in both groups, the increases were lower for HGH (human growth hormone), cortisol, prolactin, and noradrenaline among music group patients. Subjective evaluation revealed that perioperative anxiety was greatly decreased by the music. Ten of the 15 music subjects experienced sleep while only 3 of 15 control subjects slept and 8 were made more anxious by operating room sounds (Tanioka, et al., 1985). The results were nearly identical to those obtained by Oyama et al. (1983) in their study of anxiolytic music and endocrine function in surgical patients.

In a similar study of the effects of music in operations that utilize regional anaesthesia, 48 male neurological patients between the ages of 40 and 90 were premedicated with a mixture of dilantin and atropene. This was followed by either music through headphones *or* diazepam. The music was generally slow and soft with restrained dynamics, small intervals, even descending and ascending melodic contour, and nonsyncopated rhythm. It was found that the degree of anxiolytic sedation in the music group was equal to that of the pharmacological group (diazepam), but without undesirable side effects (Sehhati-Chafai & Kau, 1985).

Because music has been found effective in a variety of hospital applications, the question often arises concerning the effectiveness of recorded music as compared to live music. In a representative investigation of this question, Bailey (1983) studied 50 hospitalized cancer patients between the ages of 17 and 69. Each subject listened to 25 minutes of live or tape recorded music. Tension-anxiety and vigor were measured before and after the music using the Profile of Mood States (POMS) questionnaire and a questionnaire designed by the investigator. Subjects who heard live music reported significantly less tension-anxiety, more vigor, more changes in physical discomfort, more changes in mood, and more mood changes for the better than did the subjects in the taped music group. It was stated that the human element in live music was believed to be the important factor in affecting anxiety.

When studying anxiolytic effects of music in dental patients, Oyama et al. (1983) tested fifty subjects, each of whom served as their own control by undergoing at least two separate minor procedures. They listened to music from 10 minutes prior to the procedure until 15 minutes after the treatment ended. Periodic blood samples were drawn and tested for ACTH, HGH, prolactin, beta-endorphin, and cortisol. There was subjective evaluation also which revealed that 88% of the patients reported pretreatment anxiety and fear. With music, 16% experienced complete elimination of anxiety, and 84% felt a moderate decrease in fear. Pulse rate and mean arterial blood pressure also were measured, and both were found to be significantly lower than during control readings. Among the hormonal samplings, plasma ACTH decreased significantly at the end of dental treatment and 15 minutes after treatment as compared to control treatment conditions. Plasma growth hormone levels increased during and after dental procedures, although the music treatment levels were lower. Plasma prolactin levels also were lower with music. There were no appreciable differences in plasma cortisol and beta-endorphin levels between music and no-music treatments.

BIOMEDICAL MUSIC THERAPY
WITH PSYCHOTIC DISORDERS

When a prolonged state of anxiety leads to a condition of sustained stress, it can result in behavior change that manifests itself as diminished coping capacity. When this occurs, the individual is often labeled with an official diagnosis that indicates a mental disorder. Pratt (1993) has cited work that proposes a link between mental disease, immunologic reactions, and the psychic effects of corticosteroids, thyroid hormones, progesterone, the amines and their blockers. The relationship between dopamine, a monoamine, and its blockers and mental illness is discussed below.

Perhaps the most widely known and least understood of all mental disorders is schizophrenia. In the past, this condition was thought to apply to a person exhibiting a split personality or a behavior disorder characterized by a chronic loss of touch with reality. More recent literature, however, identifies schizophrenia as "a brain disease, now definitely known to be such. It is a real scientific and biological entity" (Torrey, 1983, p. 2). It exhibits symptoms of a brain disease such as impaired thinking, delusions, hallucinations, emotional changes, and altered behavior.

Carlson (1992) describes positive and negative symptoms of schizophrenia as those that are known respectively by their presence or their absence. Positive symptoms include thought disorders such as disorganized or irrational thinking, delusions consisting of beliefs that are contrary to fact, and hallucinations that appear as stimuli that are not actually presented by the external environment. Negative symptoms include flat affective responses, diminished speech capacity, lack of perseverance, decreased ability to experience pleasure, and social withdrawal.

Evidence has recently accrued to support a theory of causation known as the dopamine hypothesis. This theory suggests that schizophrenia is caused by overactivity of dopaminergic neurons in the brain. The hypothesis is supported by evidence showing that drugs which block dopamine receptors or interfere with dopaminergic transmission have the antipsychotic effect of reducing the symptoms of schizophrenia. Conversely, drugs that act as dopamine agonists produce positive symptoms of the disease by blocking the recovery of dopamine or by stimulating dopamine synthesis. Dopamine agonists include amphetamine, cocaine, methylphenidate, and L-DOPA.

The dopamine hypothesis and related findings concerning the effects of certain drugs on positive symptoms lend strong support to the conceptualization of schizophrenia as a neurological disorder, a brain disease, not an emotional disturbance. Further support comes from an examination of the conditions that mediate negative symptoms. Unlike positive symptoms, negative symptoms are not unique to schizophrenia. They are quite similar to those found with brain damage and there is much evidence suggesting that negative symptoms are a result of brain damage.

There are many studies that have found evidence of brain abnormalities in the computerized tomography (CT) and magnetic resonance imaging (MRI) scans of schizophrenic subjects. A rather frequent finding is that the relative size of the lateral ventricles in the brains of schizophrenic patients may be as much as twice the size of the ventricles in normal control subjects. It is believed that the most likely cause of the enlarged ventricle space is loss of brain tissue. Other areas that have been shown through research to exhibit loss of brain tissue are the frontal lobes, anterior temporal lobes, and hypothalamus. Possible causes of the damage are still under investigation. However, the damaged areas are those responsible for rationality, motor planning, emotional behavior, and associative thinking, all of which may be impaired in schizophrenia.

Ruud (1978) describes psychotic patients as inattentive, distractible, confused, depressed, hallucinated or in such an anxiety state that verbal contact is ineffective. Music makes contact through the thalamus which relays sensations and feelings directly to the emotional centers—the hypothalamus and limbic system—thereby reaching cranial emotional centers without prior need for higher cortical analysis of the sensation.

In a psychoanalytically based explanation of the therapeutic effects of music on autistic and schizophrenic children, Hudson (1973) described the autistic ego as not having developed, and the schizophrenic child as having developed with a distorted ego. He then characterized rhythm in music as a language having physiological appeal in the process of ego restructuring with autistic and schizophrenic children. The neurophysiological mechanism for this effect was addressed in Roederer's (1975) discussion of the psychophysics of music when he theorized that "the propagation through neural tissue of a cyclically changing flux of neural signals triggered by rhythmic sound patterns may...enter into resonance with the natural clocks of the brain that control body functions and behavioral response" (p. 165).

To bring psychotic patients into contact with the reality of their immediate external environment, it is often effective to involve them in active interaction with that environment. Through playing, singing, or otherwise participating in the production of music itself, the brain must act in direct relationship to the concurrent musical stimuli that enter the realm of neurological perception. Participation in a musical act requires behavior based on adequate perception of tempo, key center, rhythmic patterning, musical selection, and numerous other basic as well as more subtle aspects of the musical product. Such behaviors preclude conscious reaction to hallucinatory, delusional, or disorganized thought patterns that are characteristic of the schizophrenic patient. Sustained musical interaction, therefore, may be quite effective in helping the brain of the psychotic person regain its ability to receive, organize, and react appropriately to sensations perceived from the external environment. Future research may reveal a relationship between musical responsivity, dopamine levels, and schizoid symptomatology.

BIOMEDICAL MUSIC THERAPY FOR REVERSAL
OF SUICIDAL BEHAVIOR

Suicidal behavior has been considered to be a major indicator of severe depression. The depressive reaction is a primary personality pattern of the suicidal patient. Overt signs of depression often precede the appearance of suicidal behavior. However, some suicides are elicited by events that are not related to depression, such as avoidance of an intensely painful event or the immediate need to save the life of another person.

The type of depression for which treatment is described in this section is severe clinical depression accompanied by suicidal acts. The individual who exhibits this illness is subject to insomnia, loss of appetite and weight, and usually is tired and unable to make decisions or to get things done. Feelings of worthlessness and hopelessness are continuous. Studies show that up to 15% of those who are clinically depressed succeed in their attempts to exit through suicide.

Numerous theories have appeared attempting to explain the behavioral or biological basis for suicidal behavior. One such theory was the "aggression-turned-inward" model which held that negative emotions such as hostility or anger, generated by unfavorable events, result in aggressive drives directed toward oneself in the absence of an appropriate external object. Another theory based on change in psychological state is the "object loss" model which suggests that extremely low self esteem results from the disruption of an attachment bond when a loved one is lost, or when the individual loses a symbolic possession such as social status or one's values.

A third theoretical position known as the "reinforcement" model proposed that depressive behavior follows the loss of a major source of reinforcement. It serves to draw attention and sympathy through expressing chronic frustration from overwhelming environmental stresses. The sympathetic attention is itself reinforcing and is substituted for the reinforcement no longer available from the previous source. According to this model, the patient comes to believe that the behaviors that elicit the most reinforcing sympathy are those which take the form of suicidal acts. The three types of depression described so far may be referred to as "reactive depression" because they occur in reaction to events perceived by the person.

When the depression appears as an intrinsic personality trait independent of environmental stimuli, it is referred to as "endogenous depression" (Carlson, 1992). A fourth model of depression is considered by some to offer a viable explanation for endogenous depression. It focuses on biochemical reactions manifested by depletion of neurotransmitters known as monoamines. A widely accepted current theory is that depression has a medical basis, occurring when these substances are not present in sufficient quantities between nerve cells to facilitate passage of nerve impulses across synapses. In depression, release of some neurotransmitters, particularly serotonin, is blocked by other chemicals. As a result the person exhibits abnormalities in appetite, sleep, arousal, motivation, concentration, and many other abilities and activities.

In addition to depression, low CSF levels of serotonin (5-HT) and 5-HIAA, a product of 5-HT breakdown, are found among subjects with high levels of aggression. Among suicidal patients who are not depressed, hyper-aggressive tendencies are a frequent finding in conjunction with personality disorders. The depression-aggression-suicide relationship to serotonin assumes more significance in view of findings showing that serotonin levels among depressives with histories of violent suicide are even lower than serotonin measures among nonviolent suicidal depressives (Roost, 1995).

Without suggesting that an answer has been found to the question concerning the etiology of suicidal depression, the theoretical basis for the music therapy procedure described below takes into account all four of the etiological positions described above in this section. It is called the Expressive Emphasis Technique for reversal of suicidal behavior (Taylor, 1969). The object is not to identify or help deal with the patient's loss, nor is it to suppress attention-seeking behaviors that may attract reinforcing expressions of sympathy from others. The technique recognizes that the patient may have suffered a loss and may harbor a substantial amount of unexpressed hostility over the removal of a previously dependable source of reinforcement. The purpose is to elicit from the patient external expressions of negative, aggressive or hostile emotions and to generate feelings of reinforcement by showing him or her that those feelings will be accepted and respected when appropriately expressed.

The technique consists of an initial objective involving the use of musical expression to train the patient to be more expressive of feelings in general, and to convey the message that those feelings will be accepted by others. In this initial phase, the therapist instructs the patient to select material for active musical participation. The therapist begins by eliciting maximum expressive quality in the performance of musical ideas. Expression is pursued within a very positive atmosphere of musical enjoyment or fun and consists of exploring various interpretive techniques in order to discover the full expressive potential of each musical phrase. The patient is directed to concentrate only on expression of feelings inherent in the words or melody of each selection. As the patient becomes more comfortable with musical expression and more proficient at generating expressive ideas for performing the music, the therapist guides the choice of material to music with an increasingly greater range of expressive potential. As the musical material changes, the patient must continue to be encouraged to emphasize expression of meaning in each selection, and must never be asked to move to more expressive material unless comfortable at each current level. The therapist's role is to disapprove of any lack of full expression on the grounds that the meaning could not be conveyed to a listener. Proper expression must not be overly applauded, but must be accepted as an expected norm.

When this first phase of treatment is well established, the therapist begins to seek from the patient expression of ideas *about* the music. While maintaining the enjoyment of music as a prime feature of the patient-therapist relationship, the patient is encouraged to verbalize feelings about musical styles, compositions, or elements such as tempo or dynamics. Although expression of the patient's own emotions is not an objective at this stage, the patient may volunteer such information. When this begins to happen, it should be interpreted as a signal of readiness to move on to the next level of treatment.

In the second phase, the goal is to generate expression of the patient's own emotions. The specific objective involves expression of emotions generated *by* the music. A readily available source of musical material is the very music that is being worked on at a given time. The therapist should casually ask the patient to state verbally what feelings or emotions were experienced while singing, playing, or listening to a musical selection. Other techniques include instructing the patient to express feelings through musical improvisation, creative movement or drawing in response to musical stimuli. The latter activities are followed by discussion of perceptions and emotions that were elicited during the experience. All expressions must be accepted without judgment in order for the therapist to convey the idea that externally expressed feelings, opinions, and emotions will be accepted and respected by others.

When the patient becomes sufficiently accustomed to expressing emotions and begins voluntarily to express personal feelings, it is time for the third and most important phase of treatment. Its goal is to foster external expression of hostile emotions to replace the patient's inclination to invert such expression resulting in extremely hostile acts directed toward oneself. The objective is to motivate the patient to express negative and hostile emotions about events that may occur during the music therapy session. While continuing to portray musical enjoyment as a prime objective of the therapeutic experience, the therapist creates small instances of discomfort for the patient within the musical situation. Examples include such acts as beginning a session late but ending on time which shortens the total time of an otherwise enjoyable musical experience, playing an accompaniment too slow or too fast, losing sheet music temporarily, or mild disapproval of a song selection. As the patient attempts to regain the positive atmosphere that existed originally, the previously learned self-expression will take the form of self-assertion through expression of feelings and opinions designed to correct the discomforting elements that have been introduced. When the patient does express feelings of discomfort or a desire for change in the therapist's behavior, these expressions must be accepted without fanfare, and adjustments granted when the expressions are clearly stated to the therapist in an appropriate manner.

At this stage in the treatment, the therapist must be prepared for, and must actively seek to receive from the patient outward expressions of hostile emotions. By gradually increasing the number and intensity of discomforting elements within the musical situation, the patient can be motivated to express hostile feelings outwardly toward an appropriate object and in an acceptable manner. As these expressions occur, the patient's requests must be accepted and fulfilled in order to instill confidence in external expression of negative emotions as an effective coping mechanism. When the patient is finally able to verbally express the full range of negative emotions that had previously been directly inwardly, it will be important for the therapist to allow the original positive musical atmosphere to be regained. This is a vital step to demonstrate the value of this new coping technique.

In applying the expressive emphasis procedure with actual patients, it is found that the frequency of suicidal episodes decreases throughout treatment and reaches zero at or near the start of the third phase. Personality traits such as extraversion, self-confidence and motivation begin to reappear during music therapy sessions and to generalize as the procedure progresses. The positive feeling states reflected in the patient's behavior are brought on both by the release of negative emotions and by the reinforcing realization of effective self expression. The neuronal impulses stimulated by these awarenesses serve as monoamine agonists, resulting in reactivation of neuronal circuits that had been unable to produce these neurotransmitters in amounts sufficient to avert the suicidal depressive reaction. Because suicidal depression has been shown to be associated with decreased levels of monoamine neurotransmitters such as serotonin, it is believed that future research will demonstrate that the disappearance of suicidal behavior is reflected in the recovery of normal monoamine production in the central nervous system.

VIII

CONCLUSION

REDISCOVERING
MUSIC THERAPY

Is music therapy a professional discipline? Does it stand as an independently justifiable profession within the arena of medical practice? Throughout most of the twentieth century, music therapists have claimed and sought professional status while admitting apologetically that there is no known and agreed-upon explanation for the positive therapeutic effects that are obtained. The activities could be listed, the settings and patient populations could be described, and the outcomes of music therapy intervention could be reported with confidence. Also cited have been the many other intervention procedures with which music therapy has allied itself, such as behaviorism, psychoanalysis, guided imagery, rational emotive therapy, transactional analysis, and Gestalt therapy to name a few. Even with an expanding body of research showing positive therapeutic effects of music independent of other influences, the field of music therapy has not been able to incorporate these reports into an integrated independent philosophy of music therapy that everyone could agree upon.

By adopting an interdisciplinary view of the theoretical basis for music therapy, it is possible to discover countless correlates between the effects of music and findings from other fields about the realities of human behavior. Much of the research in other disciplines involves direct investigation of the effects of music as a variable. What emerges from such an interdisciplinary overview is the realization that the vast majority of those studies involve attempts to understand the workings of the human brain. Because the brain is central to music and to nearly all other observable human behavior, it must therefore be a major focus of any comprehensive theory of music therapy. The advantage is that brain functions can be studied and reported scientifically instead of continuing to rely on claims of the "magical" or "mystical" power of music. Such claims have led to a general impression that the value of music as therapy is its ability to change moods, to calm or stimulate patients, or to provide material that can be described as only symbolic rather than specific. Beyond that impression, the ancient belief persists in the ability of music to assist in invoking or confronting spiritual forces as part of the healing process. Still another belief system held by some is based on the idea that music is a part of the sound that is a universal energy force having the power to heal through relating to "chakras" of the body.

In the abstract of his presentation to the Seventh World Congress of Music Therapy in 1993, Professor Leonord De Alemann of the University of El Salvador proclaimed his annoyance at hearing the power of music referred to as "magical," especially since it has been explained scientifically. Modern music therapists are rediscovering music as therapy through investigations of its direct effects on the human nervous system. The relationship, for example, between music and movement is being investigated from a new perspective in studies such as those conducted by Thaut (1991) et al. The theoretical perspective of the investigation, including the interpretation of its findings, involved more than a report of musical activities and therapeutic results. The observed connections between music and human function are discussed and interpreted through their relationship to other findings reported in such sources as *Experimental Brain Research, Behavioural Brain Research, Brain Research, Canadian Journal of Physiology and Pharmacology,* and *Electroencephalography and Clinical Neurophysiology.* The discussion includes such systems as the reticulospinal tract, cerebellum, and the red nucleus of the midbrain, and mentions electromyographic indicators of activity in specific muscles and muscle groups. The clinical considerations reported for the results tend to encourage therapists to approach movement objectives with stroke and traumatic brain injury patients from the viewpoint of using music as a neurological entrainment mechanism rather than simply as a way to stimulate movement.

Medical doctors have also been major participants in the building of a scientific relationship between music and neurology as a basis for music therapy. Lee, Spintge, Droh, Oyama and Wilson are examples of physicians who have become leaders in producing the growing body of research that is establishing the brain as the important link between musical effects and human responses. In his discussion of the biology of music, Wilson (1989) mentions the role of basal ganglia in task learning, and cites studies showing that responses in the dentate nucleus of the cerebellum preceded activation of neurons in the precentral (motor) cortex by as much as 33 msec. Wilson went on to predict a much closer relationship between brain science and music.

Through the new and growing relationship between music and neurology, a rediscovery of the function of music as therapy is taking place. Investigators and practitioners are realizing that the therapeutic role of music in clinical applications is much broader and more important than previously thought. Its effects are much more specific, describable, and predictable than past therapists dared claim. Future therapists who are well versed in biomedical theory and who remain current with recent findings, will be able to describe in detail musical effects that have been previously considered mystical and incapable of being analyzed or explained. The new knowledge, when viewed collectively, leads to a redefinition of music therapy as a discipline with the human brain as its central focus. The following is a Biomedical Definition of Music Therapy:

> Music Therapy is the enhancement of human capabilities through the planned use of musical influences on human brain functioning.

Both the Biomedical Theory and the Biomedical Definition are offered not to replace or to discount any other theoretical or philosophical position that may have been advanced concerning music therapy as a discipline. The purpose is to provide a conceptual system that is grounded in large and growing amounts of empirical evidence. This system can provide a unifying conceptual framework for many of the various theoretical positions and clinical modalities existing within music therapy. It is believed that practicing music therapists who describe their practice in relation to biomedical theory will be recognized as medical specialists functioning as equals with their professional peers.

IMPLICATIONS OF BIOMEDICAL THEORY
FOR MUSIC THERAPY PRACTITIONERS

The biomedical theory carries with it numerous implications of change in the way music therapists explain the discipline, educate and train practitioners, practice clinical procedures, and conduct research. Development of ability to function as a biomedically based music therapist must include training in neuroscience, physiological psychology, neuromusicology and other fields that will equip even the entry level practitioner for effective practice as a medical professional. All presently required areas of musicianship continue to be necessary within a framework of biomedical music therapy. However, required competencies would include the need to demonstrate much greater knowledge of neurophysiological parameters that respond to music, and the ability to bring about positive changes in those parameters using musical experiences. Credentialing procedures and requirements should include assessment techniques that measure these areas of competence prior to professional certification.

There are important and positive implications for ways in which music therapy is defined and described. Use of biomedical theory as a basis for disseminating information about music therapy applications will elevate both the profession and professionals to levels enjoyed by other medical disciplines whose applications are firmly grounded in scientifically verifiable data. It will allow music therapy to be explained using terminology and functional parameters familiar to other health and medical practitioners, and will be able to be understood on the same medically sound basis as other disciplines.

Biomedically based music therapy clinical practice must include biological parameters in assessment both upon acceptance of a case and during ongoing therapeutic intervention. Substantial data is presented in the preceding chapters showing that music therapists and others using music therapeutically have made substantial progress in developing treatment procedures that result in the biochemical and neuromuscular changes to be measured in biomedical assessment. Until unique measurement tools and techniques appropriate to music therapy are developed, biomedical assessment procedures will need to be borrowed from other clinical disciplines.

RESEARCH IN BIOMEDICAL MUSIC THERAPY

Substantial progress has been made in building a research base specific to biomedical effects of music. Donald Hodges, Director of the Institute for Music Research, and Terry Mikiten, Associate Dean of the Graduate School of Biomedical Sciences, both of the University of Texas at San Antonio, have cited seven benefits of increased knowledge about relationships between music, the brain, and human behavior. In their presentation to a 1994 conference of the

International Society for Music in Medicine, they predicted a) better understanding and appreciation of the role of music in human life, b) greater recognition that music is not just a diversion, but has a significant impact on human physiology and psychology, c) an awareness that music can have a significant positive or negative effect on human behavior, d) increased efficiency in educating people musically, e) improvements in preparing performing musicians and in dealing with their injuries, f) increased efficiency in using music to improve the quality of life for handicapped individuals, and g) expanded use of music as treatment for medical and other widely varied clinical conditions such as childbirth, brain-injury, or chronic pain.

The vast amount of research related to biomedical theory has in the past been difficult for an individual therapist to access on a continuing basis. However, at least two technology-based systems have been developed using computerized communications to provide instant access to available information. One system is the Documental Information and Communication System (DICS) for Music Therapy headquartered at the Hogeschool Nijmegen in Holland. It consists of an international computerized network connecting computers at training sites and professional associations in widely separated locations such as the U.S., Australia, and Europe. Another system is the Computer-Assisted Information Retrieval Service System (CAIRSS) available for use through the University of Texas at San Antonio. This is an ever-growing bibliographic database of music research literature containing tens of thousands of articles from medical, psychological, educational, and musical journals. It is updated regularly and access is available through the Internet.

A review of the presently available body of research reveals examples of experimental, descriptive, historical, and philosophical research, the four traditional types of research. Many of these studies can be described as "pure" research due to their examination of musical influences independent of a projected application to any specific clinical procedure. A substantial amount of the research reflects "applied" research studies that directly examine the effectiveness of musical interventions used daily in clinical applications. All such studies contribute knowledge that eventually reveals trends and recurring relationships between music and human behavior. It is these known relationships that are utilized in the clinic to elicit therapeutic change in specific patients.

QUANTITATIVE VS. QUALITATIVE RESEARCH

Still being debated is the type of research that will provide the best foundation for the use of music as therapy. *In order to establish music therapy firmly within the community of medical and scientifically based disciplines, its research base needs to consist of valid well controlled studies whose design, methodology, and analysis procedures are replicable and yield reliable results.*

Much of the research referred to above does meet that test and contributes greatly to the establishment of music therapy as a professional discipline.

There are many other published reports that describe interventions whose out-comes consist of patient or subject accounts of impressions, images, feelings or emotions that are experienced on a so-called deeper level. These accounts are compared to the musical material that was produced, often in an improvisation, or are related to the musical progressions that helped stimulate the response. While such reports and accounts are extremely helpful in understanding the therapeutic value of artistic and intuitive effects of musical experience, the out-comes are specific to each patient and yield data that is unique and unpredict-able. Because the important finding in these reports is the content or quality of the experience for each individual, there is no projected result that can be ex-pected upon future applications of the procedure being described, and no set of data that can be subjected to quantitative analysis to determine the reliability of the effects in repeated trials. Data gathering and analysis are accomplished through the intuitions, insights, judgments, and emotional reactions of the researcher. Such reports are referred to as "qualitative research" and the re-search venue is considered integral with the clinical milieu (Aigen).

Qualitative research has numerous advocates who feel that such data honors the artistic and the beautiful aspect of music that has so far been con-sidered unexplainable and mysterious. Its methodology is decided by each in-vestigator according to their personal values and ideas. The objective is to understand musical experience as a unified whole rather than in terms of the behavior of predetermined isolated variables. While such reports do honor the nature of music as an art form, there are no specific variables identified whose general behavior is known and understood by professionals in related clinical disciplines. It is not possible, therefore, to make claims of predictable therapeu-tic outcomes that would justify the inclusion of music therapy with other medi-cal interventions in a clinical setting.

"Quantitative research," perhaps because it is the established and ex-pected form of research for professional clinical disciplines, has few advocates among music therapists actively campaigning to extol its virtues. A notable exception is Sloboda (1990) who acknowledges the mystery of music and the difficulty in understanding what music is or how it affects human behavior. Sloboda also alludes to his respect for the intuitive aversion to scientific analysis of music for fear that it would lose its mystery and power. While calling for scientists to maintain their love of music and all of its aspects that escape theo-retical capture, he points out that science can offer much to musicians. By making theoretical assumptions more explicit, it can open dialogue and test assumptions through controlled investigations that result in hard data to re-place speculations.

The Biomedical Theory of Music Therapy is an attempt to do exactly what Sloboda hypothesizes. It offers conclusions that are based on substantial amounts of interdisciplinary research data. This data base has been growing for some time and some attempts have been made to list relevant studies that bear significant relationships to music as a therapeutic modality. The biomedical theory offers a framework within which to draw coordinated conclusions from disparate sources based on the behavior of human parameters that can be understood both by music therapists and by colleagues outside of the profession.

REFERENCES

Aigen, K. (1993). The music therapist as qualitative researcher. *Music Therapy, 12,* 16–39.

Alvin, J. (1978). *Music therapy for the autistic child.* London: Oxford University Press.

Alvin, J. & Warwick, A. (1991). *Music therapy for the autistic child.* 2nd ed. New York: Oxford University Press.

Babic, Z. (1993). Towards a linguistic framework of prenatal language stimulation. In T. Blum (Ed.), *Prenatal Perception, Learning and Bonding* (pp. 361–386). Hong Kong: Leanardo Publishers.

Bailey, L. M. (1983). The effects of live music versus tape-recorded music on hospitalized cancer patients. *Music Therapy, 3,* 17–28.

Bailey, L. M. (1984). The use of songs in music therapy with cancer patients and their families. *Music Therapy, 4,* 5–17.

Barclay, M. W. (1987). A contribution to a theory of music therapy: Additional phenomenological perspectives on gestalt-qualitat and transitional phenomena. *Journal of Music Therapy, 24,* 224–238.

Barrickman, J. (1989). A developmental music therapy approach for preschool hospitalized children. *Music Therapy Perspectives, 7,* 10–16.

Bartlett, D., Kaufman, D., & Smeltekop, R. (1993). The effects of music listening and perceived sensory experiences on the immune system as measured by Interleukin-1 and Cortisol. *Journal of Music Therapy, 30,* 194–209.

Bever, T. G. (1988). A cognitive theory of emotion and aesthetics in music. *Psychomusicology, 7,* 165–172.

Birbaumer, N. (1983). The psychophysiology of anxiety. In R. Spintge & R. Droh (Eds.), *Anxiety, Pain and Music in Anaesthesia* (pp. 23–30). Basel: Editiones Roches.

Boxberger, R. (1962). Historical bases for the use of music in therapy. In E. Schneider (Ed.), *Music Therapy 1961* (pp. 125–166). Lawrence, KS: The National Association for Music Therapy, Inc.

Bonny, H. (1983). Music listening for intensive coronary care units: A pilot project. *Music Therapy, 3,* 4–16.

Boxberger, R. (1963). A historical study of the National Association for Music Therapy. In E. Schneider (Ed.), *Music Therapy 1962* (pp. 133–197). Lawrence, KS: The National Association for Music Therapy, Inc.

Boyle, M. E. (1989). Comatose and head injured patients: Applications for music in treatment. In M. H. M. Lee (Ed.), *Rehabilitation, Music and Human Well-Being* (pp. 137–148). Saint Louis: MMB Music, Inc.

Bryant, D. R. (1987). A cognitive approach to therapy through music. *Journal of Music Therapy, 24,* 27–34.

Caine, J. (1991). The effects of music on the selected stress behaviors, weight, caloric and formula intake, and length of hospital stay of premature and low birth weight neonates in a newborn intensive care unit. *Journal of Music Therapy, 28,* 180–192.

Carlson, N. R. (1992). *Foundations of Physiological Psychology.* Boston: Allyn & Bacon.

Chaquico, C. (1995). Music can aid the healing process. *Billboard.* International Weekly Newspaper. April 8, p. 1.

Chetta, H. D. (1981). The effect of music and desensitization on preoperative anxiety in children. *Journal of Music Therapy, 18,* 74–87.

Christenberry, E. B. (1979). The use of music therapy with burn patients. *Journal of Music Therapy, 16,* 138–148.

Claeys, S. M., Miller, A. C., Dalloul-Rampersad, R., & Kollar, M. (1989). The role of music and music therapy in the rehabilitation of traumatically brain injured clients. *Music Therapy Perspectives, 6,* 71–76.

Clark, M., McCorkle, R., & Williams, S. (1981). Music therapy-assisted labor and delivery. *Journal of Music Therapy, 18,* 88–100.

Clynes, M. (1985). On music and healing. In R. Spintge & R. Droh (Eds.), *Music in Medicine* (pp. 3–21). Basel: Editiones Roches.

Cohen, N. S. (1988). The use of superimposed rhythm to decrease the rate of speech in a brain-damaged adolescent. *Journal of Music Therapy, 25,* 85–93.

Cohen, N. S. (1995). The effect of vocal instruction and Visi-Pitch Feedback on the speech of persons with neurogenic communication disorders: Two case studies. *Music Therapy Perspectives, 13,* 70–75.

Cook, J. D. (1981). The therapeutic use of music: a literature review. *Nursing Forum, 20,* 252–266.

Curtis, S. (1986). The effect of music on pain relief and relaxation of the terminally ill. *Journal of Music Therapy, 23,* 10–24.

Darrow, A. (1984). A comparison of rhythmic responsiveness in normal and hearing impaired children and an investigation of the relationship of rhythmic responsiveness to the suprasegmental aspects of speech perception. *Journal of Music Therapy, 21,* 44–66.

Darrow, A. (1991). An assessment and comparison of hearing impaired children's preference for timbre and music instruments. *Journal of Music Therapy, 28,* 48–59.

Darrow, A. & Gfeller, K. (1991). A study of public school music programs mainstreaming hearing impaired students. *Journal of Music Therapy, 28,* 23–39.

Davis, W. (1987). Music therapy in 19th century America. *Journal of Music Therapy, 24,* 76–87.

Denckla, M. B. (1990). The paradox of the gifted/impaired child. In F. R. Wilson & F. L. Roehmann (Eds.), *Music and Child Development* (pp. 227–240). Saint Louis: MMB Music, Inc.

Dorow, L. G. (1976). Televised music lessons as educational reinforcement for correct mathematical responses with the educable mentally retarded. *Journal of Music Therapy, 13,* 77–86.

Fry, H. J. H. (1989). Music making for the disabled: The risks and the prevention of overuse injury. In M. H. M. Lee (Ed.), *Rehabilitation, Music and Human Well-Being* (pp. 122–136). Saint Louis: MMB Music, Inc.

Eagle, C. (1985). A quantum interfacing system for music and medicine. In R. Spintge & R. Droh (Eds.), *Music in Medicine* (pp. 319–341). Basel: Editiones Roches.

Edelstein, J. E. (1989). Musical options for upper-limb amputees. In M. H. M. Lee (Ed.), *Rehabilitation, Music and Human Well-Being* (pp. 213–225). Saint Louis: MMB Music, Inc.

Ellis, A. & Grieger, R. (1977). *Handbook of rational emotive therapy.* New York: Springer.

Frisina, R. D., Walton, J. P., & Crummer, G. C. (1988). Neural basis for music cognition: neurophysiological foundations. *Psychomusicology, 7,* 99–107.

Fukuda, Y. (1993). Breathing exercises for asthmatic children: Asthma music and the asthma symphony. In R. R. Pratt (Ed.), *Music Therapy and Music Education for the Handicapped* (pp. 135–136). Saint Louis: MMB Music, Inc.

Gaston, E. T. (1951). Dynamic music factors in mood change. *Music Educators Journal, 37,* 42.

Gaston, E. T. (1964). The aesthetic experience and biological man. *Journal of Music Therapy, 1,* 1–7.

Gardner, C., Keng, L., & Ingram, M. (1987). Music therapy rehabilitation at Goldwater Memorial Hospital. *MEH Bulletin, 2,* 15–26.

Geschwind, N. (1972). Language and the brain. *Scientific American, 226,* 76–83.

Gibbons, A. C., & McDougal, D. L. (1987). Music therapy in medical technology: Organ transplants. In R. Pratt (Ed.), *The Fourth International Symposium on Music: Rehabilitation and Human Well-Being* (pp. 61–72). Basel: Editiones Roches.

Gibbons, A. C., & Tricker, R. (1987). The influence of stimulative and sedative music selections on heart rates in university students. *Journal of the International Association of Music for the Handicapped, 3,* 26–33.

Godley, C. (1987). The use of music therapy in pain clinics. *Music Therapy Perspectives, 4,* 24–28.

Hadsell, N. (1974). A sociological theory and approach to music therapy with adult psychiatric patients. *Journal of Music Therapy, 11,* 113–124.

Hadsell, N. A. & Coleman, K. A. (1988). Rett Syndrome: A challenge for music therapists. *Music Therapy Perspectives, 5,* 52–56.

Halpaap, B., Spintge, R., Droh, R., Kummert, W., & Kogel, W. (1985). Anxiolytic music in obstetrics. In R. Spintge & R. Droh (Eds.), *Music in Medicine* (pp. 145–154). Basel: Editiones Roches.

Hanser, S., Larson, S., & O'Connell, A. (1983). The effect of music on relaxation of expectant mothers during labor. *Journal of Music Therapy, 20,* 50–58.

Hanser, S. B. (1985). Music therapy and stress reduction research. *Journal of Music Therapy, 22,* 193–206.

Harvey, A. W. (1987). Utilizing music as a tool for healing. In R. R. Pratt (Ed.), *The Fourth International Symposium on Music: Rehabilitation and Human Well-Being* (pp. 73–87). Basel: Editiones Roches.

Harvey, A. W. (1992). On developing a program in musicmedicine: A neurophysiological basis for music as therapy. In R. Spintge & R. Droh (Eds.), *MusicMedicine* (pp. 71–79). Saint Louis: MMB Music, Inc.

Heimrath, J. (1994). *Healing Power of the Gong* (S. B. Weber, Trans.). Saint Louis: MMB Music, Inc.

Hodges, D. A. (1980a). Human hearing. In D. Hodges (Ed.), *Handbook of Music Psychology* (p. 43). Dubuque: Kendall/Hunt.

Hodges, D. A. (1980b). Neurophysiology and human hearing. In D. Hodges (Ed.), *Handbook of Music Psychology* (p. 195). Dubuque: Kendall/Hunt.

Hudson, W. C. (1973). Music: A physiologic language. *Journal of Music Therapy, 10,* 137–140.

Itoh, M., & Lee, M. H. M. (1989). Epidemiology of disability and music. In M. H. M. Lee (Ed.), *Rehabilitation, Music and Human Well-Being* (pp. 13–30). Saint Louis: MMB Music, Inc.

Jacobs, A. (1987). Report on a project with autistic children at Indiana University. In R. R. Pratt (Ed.), *The Fourth International Symposium on Music: Rehabilitation and Human Well-Being* (pp. 157–164). Basel: Editiones Roches.

James, M. R. (1984). Sensory integration: A theory for therapy and research. *Journal of Music Therapy, 21,* 79–88.

Kersten, F. (1989). Musical involvement of visually impaired individuals: physiological, psychological and social importance. In M. H. M. Lee (Ed.), *Rehabilitation, Music and Human Well-Being* (pp. 154–167). Saint Louis: MMB Music, Inc.

Kovacevic, M. (1993). A new perspective of psycholinguistics: Prenatal language development. In T. Blum (Ed.), *Prenatal Perception, Learning and Bonding* (pp. 331–360). Hong Kong: Leanardo Publishers.

Kovach, A. M. (1985). Shamanism and guided imagery and music: A comparison. *Journal of Music Therapy, 22,* 154–165.

Laughlin, S. A., Naeser, M. A., & Gordon, W. P. (1979). Effects of three syllable durations using the melodic intonation therapy technique. *Journal of Speech and Hearing Research, 22,* 311–320.

Lee, M. H. M., & Kella, J. J. (1989). Computerized thermography and other technological aids in the diagnosis of musicians' neuromuscular disorders. In M. H. M. Lee (Ed.), *Rehabilitation, Music and Human Well-Being* (pp. 37–56). Saint Louis: MMB Music, Inc.

Mader, S. S. (1995). *Human Biology.* Dubuque, IA: Wm. C. Brown Publishers.

Madsen, C. K., Cotter, V., & Madsen, C. H. (1968). A behavioral approach to music therapy. *Journal of Music Therapy, 5,* 69–71.

Mahlberg, M. (1973). Music therapy in the treatment of an autistic child. *Journal of Music Therapy, 10,* 189–193.

Manchester, R. A. (1988). Medical aspects of music development. *Psychomusicology, 7,* 147–152.

Mandel, S. E. (1988). Music therapy: A personal peri-surgical experience. *Music Therapy Perspectives, 5,* 109–110.

Marcus, D. (1994). Foreword. *Music Therapy, 12,* 11–17.

Marley, L. S. (1984). The use of music with hospitalized infants and toddlers: A descriptive study. *Journal of Music Therapy, 21,* 126–132.

Maultsby, M. (1977). Combining music therapy and rational behavior therapy. *Journal of Music Therapy, 14,* 89–97.

Mazziotta, J. C., Phelps, M. E., Carson, R. E., & Kuhl, D. E. (1982). Tomographic mapping of human cerebral metabolism: Auditory stimulation. *Neurology, 32,* 921–937.

McDonnell, L. (1984). Music therapy with trauma patients and their families on a pediatric service. *Music Therapy, 4,* 55–63.

Meyer, L. B. (1967). *Music, the Arts and Ideas.* Chicago, IL: University of Chicago Press.

Michel, D. E., & Chesky, K. S. (1994). "Standards" in music and music vibration for pain relief. *Volume of Abstracts: International MusicMedicine Symposium.* Ludenscheid, Germany: International Society for Music in Medicine.

Michel, D. E., & Chesky, K. S. (1996). Music and music vibration for pain relief. In R. R. Pratt & R. Spintge (Eds.), *MusicMedicine, Vol. 2* (pp. 218–226). Saint Louis: MMB Music, Inc.

Miluk-Kolasa, B. (1993). Effects of listening to music on selected physiological variables and anxiety level in pre-surgical patients. Unpublished Doctoral Dissertation, Medical University of Warsaw.

Montello, L. (1992). Exploring the causes and treatment of music performance stress: A process-oriented group music therapy approach. In R. Spintge & R. Droh (Eds.), *MusicMedicine* (pp. 284–297). Saint Louis: MMB Music, Inc.

Morton, L. L., Kershner, F. R., & Siegel, L. S. (1990). The potential for therapeutic applications of music on problems related to memory and attention. *Journal of Music Therapy, 27,* 195–208.

Mueller, K. H. (1964). The aesthetic experience and psychological man. *Journal of Music Therapy, 1,* 8–10.

Nagler, J. C., & Lee, M. H. M. (1989). Music therapy using computer technology. In M. H. M. Lee (Ed.), *Rehabilitation, Music and Human Well-Being* (pp. 226–241). Saint Louis: MMB Music, Inc.

Noy, P. (1966). The psychodynamic meaning of music, Part I. *Journal of Music Therapy, 3,* 126–134.

Noy, P. (1967). The psychodynamic meaning of music, Parts II–V. *Journal of Music Therapy, 4,* 7–23, 45–51, 81–94, 128–131.

Oepen, G., & Berthold, H. (1985). Frequency and type of amusia following different cerebral lesions. In R. Spintge & R. Droh (Eds.), *Music in Medicine* (pp. 177–195). Basel: Editiones Roches.

Olds, J. (1956). Pleasure centers in the brain. *Scientific American, 195*(4), 105–116.

Ostwald, P. F. (1990) Music in the organization of childhood experience and emotion. In F. R. Wilson & F. L. Roehmann (Eds.), *Music and Child Development* (pp. 11–26). Saint Louis: MMB Music, Inc.

Oyama, T., Sato, Y., Kudo, T., Spintge, R., & Droh, R. (1983). Effect of anxiolytic music on endocrine function in surgical patients. In R. Spintge & R. Droh (Eds.), *Anxiety, Pain and Music in Anaesthesia* (pp. 147–152). Basel: Editiones Roches.

Oyama, T., Hatano, K., Sato, Y., Kudo, T., Spintge, R., & Droh, R. (1983). Endocrine effect of anxiolytic music in dental patients. In R. Spintge & R. Droh (Eds.), *Anxiety, Pain and Music in Anaesthesia* (pp. 143–146). Basel: Editiones Roches.

Parente, A. B. (1989). Feeding the hungry soul: Music as a therapeutic modality in the treatment of anorexia nervosa. *Music Therapy Perspectives, 6,* 44–48.

Panthuraamphorn, C. (1993). Prenatal infant stimulation program. In T. Blum (Ed.), *Prenatal Perception, Learning and Bonding* (pp. 187–220). Hong Kong: Leanardo Publishers.

Perez, M. (1989). Music, emotions, and hospitalized children. In M. H. M. Lee (Ed.), *Rehabilitation, Music and Human Well-Being* (pp. 242–252). Saint Louis: MMB Music, Inc.

Pollack, N. J., & Namazi, K. H. (1992). The effect of music participation on the social behavior of Alzheimer's disease patients. *Journal of Music Therapy, 29,* 54–67.

Pratt, R. R., & Jones, R. W. (1985). Music and medicine: A partnership in history. In R. Spintge & R. Droh (Eds.), *Music in Medicine* (pp. 307–318). Basel: Editiones Roches.

Pratt, R. R. (1988). Report on 1988 seminar "Comprehensive training programs in music therapy and music in special education throughout the world." *International Journal of Music Education, 12,* 58–59.

Pratt, R. R. (1989). A brief history of music and medicine. In M. H. M. Lee (Ed.), *Rehabilitation, Music and Human Well-Being* (pp. 1–12). Saint Louis: MMB Music, Inc.

Pratt, R. R. (1993). Music therapy and special music education: Interdisciplinary research and clinical practice with the fields of medicine and psychotherapy. In R. R. Pratt (Ed.), *Music Therapy and Music Education for the Handicapped.* (pp. 52–63). Saint Louis: MMB Music, Inc.

Pribram, K. H. (1971). *Languages of the Brain.* Englewood Cliffs, NJ: Prentice-Hall.

Prickett, C. A., & Moore, R. S. (1991). The use of music to aid memory of Alzheimer's patients. *Journal of Music Therapy, 28,* 101–110.

Rider, M. S., Floyd, J. W., & Kirkpatrick, J. (1985). The effect of music, imagery, and relaxation on adrenal corticosteroids and the re-entrainment of circadian rhythms. *Journal of Music Therapy, 22,* 46–58.

Rider, M. S. (1985). Entrainment mechanisms are involved in pain reduction, muscle relaxation, and music-mediated imagery. *Journal of Music Therapy, 22,* 183–192.

Roederer, J. G. (1985). Neuropsychological processes relevant to the perception of music—An introduction. In R. Spintge & R. Droh (Eds.), *Music in Medicine* (pp. 61–86). Basel: Editiones Roches.

Roederer, J. G. (1975). *Introduction to the Physics and Psycho-physics of Music.* New York: Springer-Verlag.

Rogers, S. J. (1990). Theories of child development and musical ability. In F. R. Wilson & F. L. Roehmann (Eds.), *Music and Child Development* (pp. 1–10). Saint Louis: MMB Music, Inc.

Roost, J. (1995). Towards an integrated model of suicide. *The Harvard BRAIN, 2,* Harvard Undergraduate Society for Neuroscience, 3–4.

Rudenberg, M. T., & Royka, A. M. (1989). Promoting psychosocial adjustment in pediatric burn patients through music therapy and child life therapy. *Music Therapy Perspectives, 7,* 40–43.

Rudenberg, M. T., & Christenberry, A. R. (1993). Promoting psychological adjustment in pediatric burn patients through music therapy and child life therapy. In R. R. Pratt (Ed.), *Music Therapy and Music Education for the Handicapped.* (pp. 164–165). Saint Louis: MMB Music, Inc.

Ruud, E. (1978). *Music Therapy and its Relationship to Current Treatment Theories.* Saint Louis: MMB Music, Inc.

Saperston, B. (1973). The use of music in establishing communication with an autistic mentally retarded child. *Journal of Music Therapy, 10,* 184–188.

Scarantino, B. A. (1987). *Music Power.* New York: Dodd, Mead & Company.

Schuster, B. L. (1985). The effect of music listening on blood pressure fluctuations in adult hemodialysis patients. *Journal of Music Therapy, 22,* 146–153.

Sears, M. L., & Sears, W. W. (1964). Abstracts of research in music therapy. *Journal of Music Therapy, 1,* 33–60.

Sears, W. W. (1951). Postural response to recorded music. Unpublished Masters Thesis, University of Kansas.

Sears, W. W. (1958). The effect of muscle on muscle tonus. In E. T. Gaston (Ed.), *Music Therapy 1957* (pp. 199–205). Lawrence, KS: McGraw-Hill.

Sehhati-Chafai, G., & Kau, G. (1985). Comparative study on the anxiolytic effect of diazepam and music in patients during operations in regional anesthesia. In R. Spintge & R. Droh (Eds.), *Music in Medicine* (pp. 231–236). Basel: Editiones Roches.

Sekeles, C. (1988). Convergent points between music and medicine as reflected in a number of examples in medieval Islamic and Judaic history. *Journal of the International Association of Music for the Handicapped, 3,* 14–24.

Semelka, G. (1983). Music as an aid in the anesthesiological practice of a general hospital. In R. Spintge & R. Droh (Eds.), *Anxiety, Pain and Music in Anesthesia* (pp. 105–109). Basel: Editiones Roches.

Shapiro, A. G., & Cohen, H. (1983). Auxiliary pain relief during suction curettage. In R. Spintge & R. Droh (Eds.), *Anxiety, Pain and Music in Anesthesia* (pp. 89–93). Basel: Editiones Roches.

Shetler, D. J. (1990). The inquiry into prenatal musical experience. In F. R. Wilson & F. L. Roehmann (Eds.), *Music and Child Development* (pp. 44–62). Saint Louis: MMB Music, Inc.

Silber, F. & Hes, J. (1995). The use of songwriting with patients diagnosed with Alzheimer's disease. *Music Therapy Perspectives, 13,* 31–34.

Skille, O. (1992). Vibro-acoustic research. In R. Spintge & R. Droh (Eds.), *MusicMedicine* (pp 253–254). Saint Louis: MMB Music, Inc.

Slabey, V. (1985). *Music Involvement for Nursing Homes.* Durand, WI: Mt. Matthew Press.

Sloboda, J. Music as a language. In F. R. Wilson & F. L. Roehmann (Eds.), *Music and Child Development* (pp. 28–43). Saint Louis: MMB Music, Inc.

Sparks, R. W., & Holland, A. (1976). Method: Melodic intonation therapy for aphasia. *Journal of Speech and Hearing Disorders, 61,* 287–297.

Spintge, R., & Droh, R. (1983). *Anxiety, Pain and Music in Anesthesia.* Basel: Editiones Roches.

Spintge, R., & Droh, R. (1985). *Music in Medicine.* Basel: Editiones Roches.

Spintge, R., & Droh, R. (1987). Effects of anxiolytic music on plasma levels of stress hormones in different medical specialties. In R. Pratt (Ed.), *The Third International Symposium on Music: Rehabilitation and Human Well-Being* (pp. 88–101). Lanham, MD: University Press of America.

Spintge, R. K. W. (1989). The anxiolytic effects of music. In M. H. M. Lee (Ed.), *Rehabilitation, Music and Human Well-Being* (pp. 82–97). Saint Louis: MMB Music, Inc.

Spintge, R., & Droh, R. (1992). Toward a research standard in musicmedicine/music therapy: A proposal for a multimodal approach. In R. Spintge & R. Droh (Eds.), *MusicMedicine* (pp. 345–349). Saint Louis: MMB Music, Inc.

Standley, J. M. (1986). Music research in medical/dental treatment: Meta-analysis and clinical applications. *Journal of Music Therapy, 23,* 56–122.

Staum, M. J. (1983). Music and rhythmic stimuli in the rehabilitation of gait disorders. *Journal of Music Therapy, 20,* 69–87.

Tanioka, F., Takazawa, T., Kamata, S., Kudo, M., Matsuki, A., & Oyama, T. (1985). Hormonal effect of anxiolytic music in patients during surgical operations under epidural anaesthesia. In R. Spintge & R. Droh (Eds.), *Music in Medicine* (pp. 285–290). Basel: Editiones Roches.

Taylor, D. B. (1969). Expressive Emphasis in the Treatment of Intropunitive Behavior. *Journal of Music Therapy, 6,* 41–43.

Taylor, D. B. (1973). Subject responses to precategorized stimulative and sedative music. *Journal of Music Therapy, 10,* 86–94.

Taylor, D. B. (1981). Music in general hospital treatment from 1900–1950. *Journal of Music Therapy, 18,* 62–73.

Taylor, D. B. (1988). Therapeutic musicians or musical physicians: The future is at stake. *Music Therapy Perspectives, 5,* 86–93.

Taylor, D. B. (1989). A neuroanatomical model for the use of music in the remediation of aphasic disorders. In M. H. M. Lee (Ed.), *Rehabilitation, Music and Human Well-Being* (pp. 168–178). Saint Louis: MMB Music, Inc.

Taylor, D. B. (1990). Childhood sequential development of rhythm, melody and pitch. In F. R. Wilson & F. L. Roehmann (Eds.), *Music and Child Development* (pp. 241–253). Saint Louis: MMB Music, Inc.

Taylor, D. B. (1993). Report from Tokyo: Arts medicine. *NAMT Notes.* (Fall), 5.

Thaut, M., Schleiffers, S., & Davis, W. (1991). Analysis of EMG activity in biceps and triceps muscle in an upper extremity gross motor task under the influence of auditory rhythm. *Journal of Music Therapy, 28,* 64–88.

Thaut, M., Brown, S., Benjamin, J., & Cooke, J. (1994). Rhythmic facilitation of movement sequencing: Effects on spatio-temporal control and sensory modality dependence. In R. R. Pratt & R. Spintge (Eds.), *MusicMedicine, Vol. 2* (pp. 104–109). Saint Louis: MMB Music, Inc.

Thompson, R. F. (1967). *Foundations of Physiological Psychology.* New York: Harper & Row.

Torrey, E. F. (1983). *Surviving Schizophrenia: A Family Manual.* New York: Harper & Row Publishers, Inc.

Ventre, M. (1994). Guided imagery and music in process: The interweaving of the archetype of the mother, mandala, and music. *Music Therapy, 12,* 19–38.

Verdeau-Pailles, J. (1985). Music and the body. *MEH Bulletin, 1,* 8–21.

Walton, J. P., Frisina, R.D., Swartz, I. P., Hantz, E., & Crummer, G. C. (1988). Neural basis for music cognition: Future directions and biomedical implications. *Psychomusicology, 7,* 127–138.

Wang, R. P. (1968). Psychoanalytic theories and music therapy practice. *Journal of Music Therapy, 5,* 114–116.

Ward, D. (1993). Aesthetic education, therapy, and children with special needs. In R. R. Pratt (Ed.), *Music Therapy and Music Education for the Handicapped* (pp. 112–124). Saint Louis: MMB Music, Inc.

Weinberger, N. M. (1993). Music, the brain, and science. *NAMM News Special Report.* National Association of Music Merchants.

Wilson, F. R. (1985). Music education for the handicapped: A keynote address to the fourth international symposium. *MEH Bulletin, 1,* 9–13.

Wilson, F. R. (1988). Music and medicine: an old liason, a new agenda. *Psychomusicology, 7,* 139–146.

Wilson, F. R. (1989). The biology of music. In M. H. M. Lee (Ed.), *Rehabilitation, Music and Human Well-Being* (pp. 31–36). Saint Louis: MMB Music, Inc.

Winn, B., Crowe, B., & Moreno, J. (1989). Shamanism and music therapy: Ancient healing techniques in modern medicine. *Music Therapy Perspectives, 7,* 67–71.

Wolfe, D. E. (1978). Pain rehabilitation and music therapy. *Journal of Music Therapy, 15,* 162–178.

Woodward, S. C., Guidozzi, F., Hofmeyer, G. J., Dejong, P., Anthony, J., & Woods, D. (1992). Discoveries in the fetal and neonatal worlds of music. In H. Lees (Ed.), *Music Education: Sharing Musics of the World* (pp. 58–66). New Zealand: University of Canterbury.

Woodward, S. C. (1992). The transmission of music into the human uterus and the response to music of the human fetus and neonate. Unpublished doctoral dissertation, University of Cape Town, South Africa.

INDEX